THE HOSPITAL CONSTRUCTION ACT

Evaluative Studies

This series of studies seeks to bring about greater understanding and promote continuing review of the activities and functions of the federal government. Each study focuses on a specific program, evaluating its cost and efficiency, the extent to which it achieves its objectives, and the major alternative means—public and private—for reaching those objectives. Yale Brozen, professor of economics at the University of Chicago and an adjunct scholar of the American Enterprise Institute for Public Policy Research, is the director of the program.

THE HOSPITAL CONSTRUCTION ACT

An evaluation of the
Hill-Burton program, 1948-1973

Judith R. Lave
Lester B. Lave

American Enterprise Institute for Public Policy Research
Washington, D. C.

Evaluative Studies 16, May 1974

ISBN 0-8447-3129-3

Library of Congress Catalog No. 74-80658

CONTENTS

TABLES

SUMMARY OF FINDINGS

The State of Medical-Care Delivery. If the goal of the medical-care delivery system is the improvement of health, a great deal of money has been spent with no discernible effect. Prices and expenditures have risen, but the indices of health, such as life expectancy or mortality rates, have shown no improvement.

One reason for the ineffectiveness of increased health-care expenditures is the inefficient allocation of these resources. Too much is spent on expensive inpatient care and too little on ambulatory care. More should be done to improve the basic health level of the population—for example, by improving public health, health education and people's health habits, and by cleaning the environment. Fewer resources should be put into personal health services.

Wide-ranging changes can be expected in medical-care delivery in the next ten years due to extended insurance programs, health maintenance organizations (HMOs), and more extensive government intervention. The system governing the expansion and modernization of hospitals should be flexible and should motivate hospitals to react rapidly to changes in the demand for their services.

The Hill-Burton Program. This program has been popular—widely supported by hospitals, by the health-care industry in general, and by community and national leaders.

Note: This work was supported by grants from the American Enterprise Institute for Public Policy Research, the R. K. Mellon Charitable Trusts, and the National Center for Health Services Research and Development (HS00592-02). The opinions are those of the authors and do not necessarily represent those of the sponsoring agencies. We thank Yale Brozen, Harold Granning, Edward Noroian, Peter Pashigian, and Lester Silverman for helpful suggestions. Neither they nor the sponsors are responsible for any errors that remain.

It has adapted to changing needs, shifting its emphasis from construction to modernization, from rural to poverty areas, and from general hospitals to other types of facilities. But its allocation formula could not be changed. Only the introduction of new grant programs altered the program's emphasis and allotment of funds.

The Hill-Burton program has financed a small (usually less than 15 percent) but significant proportion of annual hospital construction. The program has increased the number of hospital beds, especially in small cities, so that beds are no longer concentrated in the richer states. It has also helped hospitals to modernize, and has been influential in the development of state and regional planning for hospital care.

It has been efficient, at least in the sense that the proportion of costs spent on federal administration has been small. For example, in fiscal 1973 the federal administrative cost of providing $197 million in grants and $500 million in loans was $3.2 million. However, the program's Davis-Bacon requirement, its planning requirements, and its construction standards have caused construction costs for supported facilities to rise.

The program does not seem to have contributed to a general excess in hospital capacity, at least in the sense that occupancy rates do not seem to have fallen. Low occupancy rates in supported hospitals result from small hospital size (a bias built into the program initially) rather than from too many hospital beds. National guidelines specified that Hill-Burton funds could not be used to modernize or expand a hospital unless there was evidence that the additional beds would be used. However, those who believe there is substantial excess capacity see the Hill-Burton program as having contributed to this overcapacity, even if the decision for each hospital was a reasonable one.

The program has had a small part in reducing the importance of proprietary hospitals relative to voluntary hospitals, in the short-term hospital sector. Since the Hill-Burton program has had an effect on the distribution of hospital beds, it also has had an effect on the distribution of physicians. Some states—the low-income states, in particular—have more physicians now than they would have had in the absence of the program.

The Need for Expanding Hospitals. State and federal planning agencies and most observers agree that there is no overall deficit of hospital beds in the United States. The problem—if there is one—is that of maintaining an appropriate distribution within a state as population shifts.

Extensive hospitalization insurance and other factors such as the greater availability of beds have encouraged the overuse of inpatient facilities. Shifting utilization from inpatient to ambulatory-care facilities could yield major cost savings and reduce the demand for hospital facilities.

Modernization of existing hospitals, particularly in central cities, is an important need. Facilities are expensive, and the pace of technology makes them obsolete before they wear out.

Financing Hospital Capital Expenditures. Planning agencies (state and local) have not been successful in persuading hospitals to coordinate their capacities and specialized services. Forecasting a community's hospital needs is inherently difficult. Compounding the conventional problems of anticipating total population growth is the need to account for the special groups (defined geographically or by religion) that prefer their own special facility and are willing to pay for it.

The magnitude of capital expenditures required for hospitals exceeds the resources of traditional sources of funds: philanthropy, Hill-Burton, and extra charges for self-pay patients. The only viable source of more funds is current revenues, which means including full interest and depreciation in reimbursement from "third-party" sources such as Blue Cross. This change cannot be made without carefully designed reimbursement formulas or strict controls to prevent needless expansion.

Hospital costs have risen rapidly because most revenues come to hospitals on a "cost-plus" basis. Reimbursement patterns must be changed so that hospitals are no longer guaranteed that revenue will equal costs regardless of their productivity.

Centralizing control of hospitals through certificate-of-need requirements, budget reviews, or denial of reimbursement would only worsen inefficiency without solving the problem.

An incentive-reimbursement system is advocated to promote hospital efficiency and rationalize capital expenditures. Hospitals would be reimbursed on a case basis, taking account of the case mix of the hospital and its teaching programs. The system would be based on a formula that assured the hospital of average efficiency recovery of operating and capital costs. Deficits would force inefficient hospitals to improve their management, change the nature of their operations, or shut down.

Equity capital from private investors is an additional source of capital for modernization and expansion. While such funds could be used in conjunction with voluntary hospitals, they are most likely to be used in proprietary hospitals, making the establishment of a fair reimbursement system of great importance for both types of institutions.

The incentive-reimbursement system would eliminate one of the major complaints against proprietary hospitals—that they take cases that are relatively cheap to treat, leaving nonprofit hospitals with the more expensive cases. The incentive-reimbursement system would pay a hospital in relation to its case mix.

Recommendations on the Hill-Burton Program. We agree with President Nixon's recommendation that the Hill-Burton program should be terminated, the federal agency disbanded, and some activities shifted to other agencies.

No more grants or loan guarantees for construction or modernization should be made.

The financial state of hospitals in ghetto areas should be investigated. If the number of "free-care patients" (those not able to pay and not covered by Medicare, Medicaid, or insurance) poses a problem, federal or local governmental support should be provided to pay for current operations as well as capital expenditures.

Recent legislation (P.L. 92-603, generally known as H.R. 1) requires that the federal government initiate and evaluate experiments in incentive reimbursement. Because we view this method as the key to solving many financial problems, especially those of hospitals, we are concerned that the experiments be well-designed, broad, and imaginative, so that they genuinely test this technique for dealing with capital needs of hospitals and other problems as well.

INTRODUCTION

One of the most popular federal programs is the support of construction and modernization of health facilities under the Hill-Burton program. Since 1948 this program has channeled more than $3 billion in federal funds into health facilities and has assisted in building or modernizing hospitals in areas where needs were particularly acute.[1]

In the twenty-seven years since the 1946 act establishing the program, the financial climate for voluntary hospitals has undergone major change. Philanthropy is no longer a major source of funds for construction and operations. Third-party financing of hospital care, such as Blue Cross, Medicare, and Medicaid, has become the dominant source of hospital revenue, and hospitals have become enormously expensive, in terms of both construction and operating costs. Whatever goals were set for the Hill-Burton program in 1946, very different needs are salient in 1974. Indeed, the success of the Hill-Burton program in constructing hospitals has contributed to these changes.

President Nixon has stated that the Hill-Burton program has outlived its usefulness. For fiscal 1973 he recommended that no funds be appropriated for construction and modernization grants; for fiscal 1974 he recommended that the federal agency be disbanded, and its remaining functions handed over to other agencies.

As the Nixon administration and the Congress contemplate the future of this program and study the problem of financing the construction and modernization of health-care facilities, a number of questions arise.

- Has the program satisfied the goals of Congress in the 1946 legislation?

- Has the program been responsive to changes in the environment in which hospitals exist?
- What are the current needs for financing the construction and modernization of health-care facilities?
- What is the best way of meeting these needs?

We shall not try to assess whether the Hill-Burton program was ideal for meeting construction needs in 1946. Hindsight is rarely flattering and never fair. Furthermore, any major piece of legislation is a compromise, reflecting the pulling and tugging of the political process. Instead, we focus our attention on the success of the program as enacted and on the current needs for capital expenditures, particularly for short-term hospitals.

We begin with a brief history of the Hill-Burton program.[2] We trace legislative changes affecting the types of facilities eligible for support and describe the formulas developed for the allotment of federal funds. In Chapter II we report the amounts and objects of the support given, and examine whether the allocation of funds has been consistent with the stated priorities of the program. In Chapter III we try to determine the extent to which the goals in the 1946 act have been met and its effect on the distribution of hospital beds and of doctors. In Chapter IV we consider some of the general problems in the hospital industry and some of the proposed solutions, particularly as they affect capital expenditures. We conclude with some recommendations for financing future capital expenditures that differ considerably from the Hill-Burton solution.

CHAPTER I

HISTORY OF THE HILL-BURTON PROGRAM

Throughout the Depression and World War II, few hospitals were built in the United States. Many existing facilities became obsolete. According to general belief, not only was there an overall shortage of hospital beds but also existing beds were badly distributed among the states and between rural and urban areas within the states. These problems were highlighted in the 1947 Report of the Commission on Hospital Care,[1] as well as in hearings held a few years earlier by committees of both houses of Congress.[2]

To identify and meet some of the deficiencies in the amount and distribution of hospital services, Congress enacted the Hospital Survey and Construction Act of 1946 (P.L. 79-725), commonly known as the Hill-Burton program. The preamble to the act set out its major objectives:

(a) to inventory their existing hospitals . . . to survey the need for construction of hospitals and to develop programs for construction of such public and other non-profit hospitals as will, in conjunction with existing facilities, afford the necessary physical facilities for furnishing adequate hospital, clinic and similar services to all their people; and

(b) to construct public and other nonprofit hospitals in accordance with such programs.

In evaluating the program, it is important to note that construction of hospitals was an explicit goal. If there are too many beds today or too much reliance on inpatient care, the problem is due to the original act and the failure to change it, rather than to the operation of state and federal agencies.

7

The Hill-Burton program was set up not as a federally administered program but as a federal-state partnership. The Hill-Burton agency designated by each state was given an initial grant to survey hospital needs and then allotted funds to carry out its construction program subject to federal approval of the state plan. This approach involved a number of problems, including establishment of guidelines for the state agencies in developing and implementing their plans and determination of methods for allocating Hill-Burton funds among the states.

Legislative History

The law that embodied the Hill-Burton program provided that grants be given to the states for two purposes:

(1) to assist in a survey of state needs and to develop state plans for the construction of public and other voluntary nonprofit hospitals and public health centers, and

(2) to assist in building such facilities.

The original act was often amended. In 1954, for example, an amendment provided the states with grants to assist specifically in the construction of diagnostic and treatment centers (outpatient facilities), hospitals for the chronically ill (and, later, long-term care facilities), and rehabilitation centers.[3] In 1964 amendments provided funds specifically for the modernization of facilities.[4] In 1970 the grant programs were supplemented by a loan guarantee program,[5] under which, in lieu of a construction grant, the federal government pays a portion of the interest cost and acts as co-signer of loans to selected hospitals, guaranteeing the payment of principal and interest. Furthermore, the secretary of health, education and welfare can make loans to help public agencies carry out their projects for construction and modernization of health facilities.

The decision to broaden the program was a response to changing circumstances and attitudes about medical-care delivery and financing. The states, however, had to allocate funds according to the strict categories specified in the legislation. An amendment proposed by the administration in 1970 to end this categorization by allowing all Hill-Burton funds to go as a block to the states was not enacted.

Defining Need

In the development of state plans, standards of adequacy had to be applied in determining state needs. The 1946 act empowered the surgeon general to prescribe the number of general beds required for adequate hospital services for each state, not to exceed 4.5 beds per thousand population, except in sparsely populated states.

From 1946 to 1965, standards of adequacy were defined in terms of ratios of beds to population. Defining the need for hospital care in these terms came under strong criticism. Opponents argued that the figure was arbitrary and that the demand for hospital care could be quite different in areas with the same size population, so that a given bed-population ratio could mean excess capacity in some regions and crowding in others. One of the reasons that *specific* grants for modernization were established in the Harris-Hill amendments of 1964 was that Hill-Burton funds could not be distributed to regions that had more than the specified number of beds. Although urban hospitals were often obsolete and deteriorating, a city with "enough" beds could not receive assistance under the Hill-Burton program for needed renovation.

For inpatient facilities, both long-term and general, standards have become more sophisticated. The Public Health Service formula for determining need, established in 1965, incorporates three basic criteria (plus a small adjustment factor):

- population (projected for five years),
- current utilization rates (the number of bed-days actually used by the population), and
- an occupancy factor (the average percentage of beds maintained for patient care that are filled). For general hospital beds this average is 80 percent; for long-term care facilities, 90 percent.

While the more specific definition represents an improvement, it is still subject to fundamental problems. The goal of the 1946 legislation might have been stated as (1) improved health for the population together with an ability to respond to accidents, natural disasters, and other traumatic situations, and (2) construction of those hospital beds that would effectively contribute to this goal, judged in terms of their cost relative to the cost of other methods of achieving the goal. Admittedly it would have been exceedingly difficult to have defined the number of hospital beds needed. But at least with this statement of goals it would not have been possible to cite an increase in hospital beds as evidence of the legislation's success.

The danger of focusing on subgoals, such as building hospitals, must be stressed. Medical-care delivery is in a state of ferment and simple formulas for projecting need are certain to be misleading.

The rate of increase in medical-care expenditures has slowed and emphasis has shifted to ambulatory and preventive care (in order to avoid use of expensive inpatient care where possible). Indeed, there is evidence that improvements in health are more likely to come from improvements in public health services (such as innoculation programs), cleaner environment, better personal health habits and diet, and better occupational health conditions than from increased expenditures on personal health services.[6]

The same sorts of comments apply to the methods for determining needs for public health centers and outpatient facilities. In addition, the working definitions currently used are also inadequate.

For example, in determining the need for outpatient facilities, the Public Health Service pointed out that the need is greatest where there is a shortage of private physicians (not defined). It also stipulated that in counting existing outpatient facilities, offices of individuals and groups in private practice should be ignored.[7]

In assessing state needs and in developing plans for construction and modernization, the state agencies determine whether beds in existing facilities are acceptable for patient use. With the 1964 amendments, minimum standards, relating to structural and design factors affecting the safety and efficiency of operation, were developed for assessing the physical condition of each hospital. Subject to HEW approval, states may use higher standards in determining whether theirs are "conforming" beds.

Priority Areas

In the allocation of Hill-Burton funds within the states, rural areas, where the shortage of beds was greatest, were to be given priority on the theory that if they had hospital facilities, they would be more likely to attract physicians. (The notion of thirty- to fifty-bed rural hospitals was endorsed in the original hearings by the American Public Health Association.) The initial law also asked state agencies to give priority to areas with relatively low financial resources.

The rural priority came under increasing attack by urban hospitals and by organized health groups. The 1970 amendments gave priorities in hospital construction to poorer areas and, at the option of the state, to rural communities. Densely populated areas and those designated by the secretary as poverty areas were to benefit first from funds for other kinds of construction or facilities (modernization of short-term hospitals, diagnostic or ambulatory care facilities, and long-term facilities).[8]

Allotment of Federal Funds among States

Of all the Hill-Burton funds, the largest portion was designated for the construction (and, later, modernization) of facilities. Initial proposals for determining each state's allotment reflected concern that the states with the lowest per capita income had the fewest beds per capita and, by inference, the greatest need. One bill set out an allocation based on the state's population, fiscal capacity, and need for facilities. The last two criteria were difficult to measure, yet each was closely related to per capita income.

The ultimate allotment formula depended on the state's relative population and its per capita income. The latter entered the formula twice—first as a measure of the state's need and second as a measure of its fiscal capacity. Tables 1 and 2 illustrate how these factors

Table 1
ILLUSTRATIVE DETERMINATION OF ALLOTMENT PERCENTAGE

State	Per Capita Income (1)	Index of Per Capita Income [a] (2)	Half of Index of Per Capita Income (3)	Allotment Percentage [b] (4)	Allotment Percentage Squared (5)
Richest	$6,000	133	66.7	33.3	11.09
Average	4,500	100	50.0	50.0	25.00
Poorest	3,000	66	33.3	66.7	44.36

[a] Average state equals 100.
[b] 100 minus column (3).
Source: Adapted from Paul A. Brinker and Burley Walker, "The Hill-Burton Act: 1948-1954," *Review of Economics and Statistics,* vol. 54 (May 1962), pp. 208-212.

Table 2
ILLUSTRATIVE DETERMINATION OF STATE SHARES OF THE ANNUAL FEDERAL APPROPRIATION TO AID HOSPITAL CONSTRUCTION

State	Allotment Percentage Squared (1)	Population (thousands) (2)	Weighted Population [a] (3)	Share Percentage (4)	Share Amount ($ thousands) (5)
Richest	11.09	3,000	332.7	0.79	1,580
Average	25.00	3,000	750.0	1.79	3,580
Poorest	44.36	3,000	1,330.8	3.16	6,320
U.S. total	—	200,000	42,000.0	100.00	200,000

[a] Column (2) times column (1).

were used to determine the distribution of a given federal appropriation. Each state's percentage share is determined by dividing its weighted population by the total U.S. weighted population.[9] Furthermore, per capita income governed how much of a project's total cost —ranging from one-third to two-thirds—could be covered by federal funds. (The 1970 amendments permitted federal sharing up to 90 percent for facilities serving persons in a poverty area or for projects with a great potential for reducing costs.)

The 1946 formula remained in effect for construction grants for all purposes (except those for modernization, which are based on population, per capita income, and the relative need for modernization). As the disparity between low- and high-income states in numbers of beds narrowed, and as better measures of need were proposed, an effort was made to change the allotment formula.

At the 1970 hearings, Undersecretary of Health John Veneman noted: "At the time of the establishment of the formulas, some 20 years ago, no adequate measure of health facility need existed . . . the adopted formula had the effect of directing a proportionately greater percentage of available funds into the poorest states, where the problem at the time was most acute. After 20 years of the Hill-Burton program, the picture has changed. . . . Therefore we are recommending that . . . the population and per-capita-income formula should be replaced by one comprising population, per capita income . . . and an appropriate measure of facility need." [10]

Despite the pressure, however, the formula has not been changed.

Conclusion

The Hill-Burton program has responded to change through legislative action that introduced specific programs and that set new priorities at the federal level. Some features of the original law, such as the allotment formula, became outdated but proved impervious to change. However, the rigidity of the formula was moderated by the enactment of the modernization program.

For fiscal 1973, grants were made for construction as follows:

- $85 million for long-term care facilities,
- $70 million for outpatient facilities,
- $15 million for rehabilitation facilities, and
- $157 million for short-term hospitals and public health centers.

Beyond these amounts, $90 million was authorized specifically for the modernization of existing facilities.

CHAPTER II

DISTRIBUTION OF HILL-BURTON GRANTS

The Hill-Burton program provided capital funds for a number of different kinds of health facilities. While the program was not intended to be the sole source of capital for any project, the large federal share—originally up to two-thirds of total cost—was meant to support and encourage health facility construction. In this chapter we present data on the types of projects supported, their location, and the distribution of federal funds among the states. We analyze the flow of grant funds to determine whether it was in accordance with the priorities built into the program and the formulas developed to allocate the funds.

Distribution among Projects

The success of the program in providing funds for construction and modernization is evident. By June 30, 1971, 10,748 projects had been approved,[1] about one-third for new facilities and the balance for modernization (additions, alterations, and replacements).[2] The total cost was $12.8 billion, of which $3.7 billion was provided by the federal government. Table 3 shows the number of projects approved and funded by type of facility.

The table makes it clear that short-term acute, or general, hospitals received the largest share of Hill-Burton support. Because legislative changes that shifted the focus of Hill-Burton support away from short-term hospitals are relatively recent, these aggregate figures disguise their results.

Table 4 makes the shift plain, giving the distribution of projects approved under the program for fiscal 1971. In that year, only 55 percent of the funds went toward the construction and moderniza-

Table 3

HILL-BURTON PROJECTS APPROVED, BY TYPE, 1 JULY 1947–30 JUNE 1971

Type of Facility	Total Projects		Inpatient Care Beds Provided		Outpatient and Other Health-Care Facility Projects		Cost	Hill-Burton funds	
	Number	Percent	Number	Percent	Number	Percent	Total ($ thousands)	Amount ($ thousands)	Percent
Total	10,748	100.0	470,329	100.0	3,083	100.0	12,765,900	3,717,979	100.0
Short-term hospitals	5,787	53.8	344,453	73.2	131 a	4.2	9,322,392	2,635,494	70.9
Long-term care	1,733	16.1	97,358 b	20.7	—	—	1,613,808	523,111	14.1
Units in hospitals	1,097	10.2	51,983	11.1	—	—	904,409	312,499	8.4
Nursing homes	528	4.9	37,884	8.1	—	—	571,057	171,648	4.6
Chronic disease hospitals	108	1.0	7,491	1.6	—	—	138,342	38,964	1.0
Mental hospitals	198	1.8	21,034	4.5	—	—	246,734	78,493	2.1
Tuberculosis hospitals	78	.7	7,484	1.6	—	—	75,228	27,661	.7
Outpatient facilities c	1,078	10.0	—	—	1,078	35.0	708,952	204,083	5.6
Rehabilitation facilities	552	5.1	—	—	552	17.9	440,019	135,010	3.6
Public health centers	1,281	11.9	—	—	1,281	41.6	289,049	99,689	2.7
State health laboratories	41	.4	—	—	41	1.3	69,718	14,438	.4

a Public health centers built in combination with short-term hospitals and not reported as separate projects.

b Excludes 7,209 long-term care beds built in conjunction with short-term and other hospital projects, for which funds cannot be separated from total project costs. These beds are reported in the following categories of facilities: general hospitals—7,113 beds, mental hospitals—60 beds, tuberculosis hospitals—36 beds.

c Previously designated "diagnostic or treatment centers."

Source: U.S. Department of Health, Education and Welfare, *Hill-Burton Project Register* (Washington, D. C.: U.S. Government Printing Office, 1972), p. 2.

Table 4
HILL-BURTON PROJECTS APPROVED DURING FISCAL YEAR 1971, BY TYPE OF FACILITY

Type of Facility	Total Projects		Inpatient Care Beds Provided		Outpatient and Other Health-Care Facility Projects		Cost		
								Hill-Burton funds	
							Total ($ thousands)	Amount ($ thousands)	Percent
	Number	Percent	Number	Percent	Number	Percent			
Total	296	100.0	10,612	100.0	111	100.0	512,394	117,628	100.0
Short-term hospitals	113	38.2	6,594	62.1	3	2.7	321,406	64,245	54.6
Long-term care	72	24.3	3,976	37.5	—	—	83,082	27,322	23.2
Units of hospitals	44	14.9	1,673	15.8	—	—	42,245	14,002	11.9
Nursing homes	24	8.1	2,057	19.4	—	—	33,585	11,563	9.8
Chronic disease hospitals	4	1.4	246	2.3	—	—	7,252	1,757	1.5
Mental hospitals	3	1.0	42	.4	—	—	1,023	392	.3
Tuberculosis hospitals	—	—	—	—	—	—	—	—	—
Outpatient facilities [a]	49	16.6	—	—	49	44.1	65,454	13,703	11.6
Rehabilitation facilities	34	11.5	—	—	34	30.6	29,819	7,273	6.2
Public health centers	25	8.4	—	—	25	22.5	11,610	4,693	4.0
State health laboratories	—	—	—	—	—	—	—	—	—

[a] Previously designated "diagnostic or treatment centers."
Source: HEW, *Hill-Burton Project Register*, p. 4.

tion of short-term hospitals, in contrast with the 71 percent average in prior years.

Hill-Burton as a Source of Construction Funds

The fact that Hill-Burton has provided part of the support for nearly $13 billion in health facilities construction between 1948 and 1971 is not meaningful without some measure of total expenditures of this type. Between 1949 and 1962, about 30 percent of all hospital construction projects were assisted, on average, under the program; to put it another way, about 10 percent of the annual cost of all hospital construction over this period was paid directly by the federal government under the Hill-Burton program. Annual data for selected years are presented in Table 5. They show, for example,

Table 5
HILL-BURTON AS A SOURCE OF CONSTRUCTION FUNDS, SELECTED YEARS, 1949–70

Year	Hospital Construction			Medical Facility Construction	
	Total cost ($ millions)	% of total financed by Hill-Burton grants	% of Hill-Burton projects financed under Hill-Burton program	Total cost ($ millions)	% supported by Hill-Burton grants
1949	679	6.0	18.2	—	—
1953	686	10.6	26.5	—	—
1957	879	8.9	28.8	—	—
1960	1,005	15.5	47.2	—	—
1962	1,322	13.9	38.6	1,382	12.4
1966	—	—	—	1,960	8.5
1968	1,101	14.5	—	2,260	11.4
1969	1,250	14.7	—	3,056	7.2
1970	—	—	—	3,420	5.6

Source: Hospitals data for 1949-62 from U.S. Department of Health, Education and Welfare, *Trends* (Washington, D. C.: U.S. Government Printing Office, 1963), p. 35; data for 1968 from R. Foster and D. McNeil, "How Hospitals Finance Construction," *Hospitals,* Journal of the American Hospital Association, vol. 45 (July 1, 1971), p. 47, and for 1969 from "AHA Research Capsules No. 5," *Hospitals,* vol. 46 (March 1, 1972). The data for 1968 and 1969 were obtained from a survey of hospitals and underestimate the total value of hospital construction. The researchers asked for percent of total construction costs covered by federal grants, not necessarily Hill-Burton grants. The Hill-Burton grants program is, however, by far the most important federal grant program.
Medical facilities data were obtained directly from the Hill-Burton agency.

that in 1962, 13.9 percent of the total cost of hospital construction and 38.6 percent of the costs of construction of hospitals receiving some program support was financed by Hill-Burton grants. The Hill-Burton program has thus financed a small (usually less than 15 percent) but significant portion of hospital construction. Table 5 also suggests that the program was less important as a source of finance for health facilities other than hospitals.

Distribution among States

As we pointed out in Chapter I, the grant funds were not to be distributed equally among the states. The allotment formula was slanted in favor of the low-income states. Not only were they allotted more Hill-Burton funds per capita, but a higher proportion of their project costs could be financed by federal funds.[3]

Between 1948 and 1971, substantial shifts occurred among the states both in relative per capita income and in relative population. Hence the extent to which the total flow of federal funds was related to state per capita income is difficult to determine accurately. An approximate measure for each state can be devised by dividing the total amount of Hill-Burton monies received between 1948 and 1971 by its 1960 population. In Figure 1 we plot this measure for each state against 1960 per capita income. Figure 2 depicts the percentage of total project costs financed by the program against 1960 state per capita income. The diagrams show a strong inverse association between Hill-Burton support and income. The higher a state's per capita income, the lower its Hill-Burton support. A few states with low population, such as Nevada, are exceptions to this relationship because of minimum grant levels. The correlation between Hill-Burton funds per capita (over the course of the program) and 1960 income per capita is −0.78; the correlation between proportion of project supported by Hill-Burton grants and 1960 per capita income is −0.73.

The relationship between the size of the Hill-Burton grant per capita and per capita income has weakened in recent years, since the funds allocated under the modernization section of the program have not been tied so closely to per capita income as before. In 1971, the correlation between Hill-Burton funds per capita and state per capita income is −0.25; for projects receiving some Hill-Burton funds, the correlation between the proportion of costs met by federal funds and per capita income is −0.37. These much lower correlations indicate that the income redistribution effect of the program has lessened in recent years.

Figure 1

RELATION OF HILL-BURTON FUNDS RECEIVED BY STATES TO STATE INCOME, PER CAPITA BASIS, 1948-71

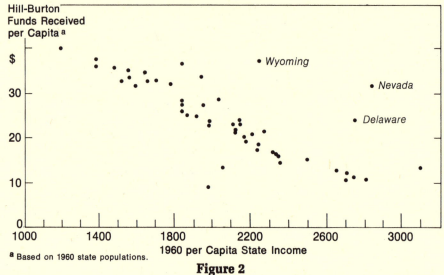

Hill-Burton Funds Received per Capita [a]

1960 per Capita State Income

[a] Based on 1960 state populations.

Figure 2

RELATION OF SHARE OF STATE PROJECT COSTS FINANCED BY HILL-BURTON TO PER CAPITA STATE INCOME, 1948-71

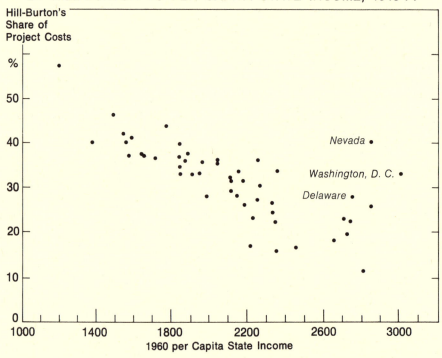

Hill-Burton's Share of Project Costs

1960 per Capita State Income

Distribution among Regions

The original act required the state Hill-Burton agency to give priority to rural and low-income areas when allocating grants. The rural priority was not incorporated in added programs, such as that for modernization, and was dropped after 1970. We would expect, therefore, that projects supported under the Hill-Burton program would tend to be concentrated in low-income and rural areas, but to a lesser extent in recent years.

Data showing the distribution of Hill-Burton hospital grants by community size (as of 1960) are shown in Table 6. The data in columns (1), (2), and (3) of this table were obtained from a one-fifth sample of short-term hospitals that received some support under the Hill-Burton program.[4] Columns (4), (5), and (6) contain data on distribution of short-term hospital projects by community size from 1968 to 1970.

The recent period does not differ significantly from the overall history of Hill-Burton. Funds continued to be concentrated in cities of 10,000 to 25,000. Over the course of the program these cities accounted for 19.8 percent of total projects and 22.0 percent of total funds. In the late sixties the share of support received by these cities decreased. Between 1968 and 1970 they undertook 15.2 percent of the projects supported under the program, built 17.6 percent of the beds constructed with Hill-Burton support, and received 17.3 percent of the funds. These numbers can be put in perspective by noting that in 1960, 9.8 percent of the population resided in communities of that size.

The focus of the program on smaller communities is evidenced by the fact that 74.8 percent of all short-term hospital projects under the program were undertaken in communities with less than 50,000 population. They received 67.2 percent of total funds. Since 63.8 percent of the 1960 population lived in these communities, the program transferred more funds per capita to the residents of smaller communities.

In the years 1968-70, legislative attention shifted to the poverty areas in large cities. Table 6 shows, however, that little of this shift took concrete form. The largest cities benefited from only a slight increase in projects and funds.

A view of the program's transfer effect can be obtained by comparing these data with the 1960 distribution of population shown in the last column of the table. Each category of city between 2,500 and 249,999 population received a share of funds greater than its proportion of population. Each received a greater amount of Hill-Burton funds per capita than areas above or below this range. Cities

19

Table 6

DISTRIBUTION OF HILL-BURTON PROJECTS AND OF POPULATION, BY COMMUNITY SIZE, 1948–71

(in percents)

1960 Community Size	Sample of Short-Term Hospitals Supported, 1948–71			Total Projects, 1968–70			1960 Population [a]
	Total number of projects	Costs met by Hill-Burton funds	Hill-Burton funds	Total number of projects	Hill-Burton funds	Inpatient beds	
Less than 2,500 and rural	14.9	37.4	7.0	17.1	9.7	9.6	36.0
2,500–4,999	14.1	30.0	9.3	13.2	9.5	9.6	4.2
5,000–9,999	14.4	32.6	12.6	15.1	14.6	14.7	5.5
10,000–24,999	19.8	29.3	22.0	15.2	17.3	17.6	9.8
25,000–49,999	11.6	25.9	16.3	9.9	12.2	12.2	8.3
50,000–99,999	6.9	33.3	9.0	7.3	8.9	9.0	7.7
100,000–249,999	7.4	23.7	10.6	8.0	9.7	9.8	6.5
250,000 and more	10.8	21.1	13.3	14.2	18.1	17.5	22.0
Total	100.0	—	100.0	100.0	100.0	100.0	100.0

[a] 5.5 percent of the population lived in unincorporated parts of urbanized areas. However, 30.1 percent of the population lived in towns smaller than 2,500, did not live in urban fringes, and did not live in unincorporated places with a population density of 1,500 per square mile or more, that is, in rural areas.

Note: Here and in subsequent tables, details may not add to totals due to rounding.

Source: Short-term hospitals data from HEW, *Hill-Burton Project Register;* inferences drawn from a one-fifth sample of hospitals ever supported. Total projects data from HEW, *Hill-Burton Progress Report,* 1 July 1947–30 June 1970, p. 23. Population data from U.S. Bureau of the Census, *Statistical Abstract of the United States, 1972* (Washington, D. C.: U.S. Government Printing Office, 1971), p. 17.

of 2,500 to 25,000 received about 150 percent more funds per capita than a proportional allocation would have called for, and the next three categories of cities (up to 250,000) together benefited 60 percent more than population alone would have called for. Cities of less than 2,500 (and rural areas) received 77 percent less funds per capita, and cities of more than 250,000 received 39 percent less than sheer numbers suggested they were entitled to. The apparently disproportionate amount received by smaller cities overstates the transfer effect since they also served the rural population.

Table 7 relates the distribution of Hill-Burton funds to the 1960 median family income of the county in which the hospital is located. It shows that 13 percent of the projects supported were undertaken in counties where the 1960 median family income was less than $3,000. While a very high proportion of construction costs of hospitals in low-income communities were financed by the federal grant, they received relatively less of the funds. The highest share of Hill-Burton monies went to short-term hospitals in middle-income communities.[5]

How Much Were Hill-Burton Funds Worth?

The total cost of the projects partially supported under the Hill-Burton program was $12.8 billion. Of this amount, $3.7 billion was

Table 7

PERCENTAGE DISTRIBUTION OF FUNDS TO SHORT-TERM HOSPITALS, BY COUNTY FAMILY INCOME, 1948–71

1960 Median Family Income of County in Which Hospital is Located	Total Projects	Hill-Burton Grant Funds	Construction Costs Financed by Hill-Burton
Less than $3,000	13.0	8.2	45.5
$4,000–$4,999	15.0	11.5	41.7
5,000– 5,999	23.0	23.6	33.7
6,000– 6,999	29.8	30.3	26.7
7,000– 7,999	13.8	17.4	21.5
8,000– 8,999	5.1	8.3	17.7
9,000– 9,999	.4	5.7	20.0
10,000 and over	0.0	0.0	0.0
Total	100.0	100.0	—

Source: Based on a one-fifth sample of short-term hospitals listed in HEW, *Hill-Burton Project Register.*

financed by grants. But the program was not in fact worth this full amount since certain restrictions raised the cost of the supported projects. How much, then, was the federal financing worth?

An answer to that question depends on the ways in which the program affected project costs and restrictions placed on future operations. First, projects assisted by Hill-Burton funds are subject to an intensive review process that can prove costly if it delays construction in an inflationary period. Second, projects assisted by Hill-Burton funds have to meet prescribed standards of construction and equipment.[6] If the standards are unreasonable, the result could be an increase in costs. Third, Hill-Burton projects, like other federally assisted construction, must conform to the Davis-Bacon Act and pay construction workers "at rates not less than those prevailing on similar work in the locality as determined by the Secretary of Labor."[7] If the prevailing wage is improperly estimated above the market, construction costs would be higher than they otherwise would have been. Finally, the grants might be used to require changes in operations, such as opening emergency rooms or obstetrical facilities or treating more "free-care" patients.

To the extent that any of these factors operates, the value of Hill-Burton monies is reduced. For a simple arithmetic example, suppose that one-third of the cost of a project could be financed by a Hill-Burton grant and that the project would cost $100 if it did not meet federal regulations, but $126 if it did so. In this case, the real value of Hill-Burton funds is not $42 but $16.

Some of these questions were considered in a study of the construction costs of health facilities conducted in 1972 by the comptroller general of the United States.[8] In an effort to find ways of reducing construction costs for facilities assisted by Public Health Service funds, the General Accounting Office first sought to determine if and how federal regulations put upward pressure on costs.

In studying the federal review processes of thirty-three construction projects, the GAO learned that the preconstruction planning period averaged six and one-half years and the estimated cost of the projects increased by about one-third over that time. It concluded, however, that the need for review by the state Hill-Burton agency or by HEW officials did not extend this period unduly.

The study also found no evidence that the Hill-Burton construction regulations, by themselves, contributed to higher costs. Indeed, the consensus of architects, hospital administrators, and government officials was that Hill-Burton "regulations constitute reasonable minimum requirements which are generally matched or exceeded by other applicable building codes or by the desires of the owners of the facilities." [9] The study reported, however, that any construction project suffers from a multiplicity of federal and nonfederal codes and regulations, often duplicative and sometimes contradictory, that increase costs and promote confusion.

While these requirements were benign, the GAO found that the Davis-Bacon requirement imposed higher costs. In an earlier study, the GAO had found that the Department of Labor had made a number of "improper" wage determinations and that construction costs of federal projects were increased by 5 to 15 percent as a result. [10] In the 1972 study, the GAO focused not on the accuracy of wage determinations, but on whether there were differences in costs between federally assisted and privately funded projects. In addition, it received many comments on wage determinations and their effects.

The minimum wages set under the Davis-Bacon requirement are usually union rates. Union contractors stated that the requirements allowed them to compete on federal projects; open shop contractors complained that the requirements increased costs by 5 to 20 percent. [11] In the Southeast, some contractors would not bid on federally assisted projects because they would have to pay higher wages than normal and because the wage classifications were restrictive. Outside metropolitan areas, where both union and nonunion wages are lower, contractors reported that the assigned wage rates were usually based on union wages in the nearest metropolitan area, contrary to the instruction in the Davis-Bacon Act that the "prevailing wage is to be measured in the political subdivision in which the work is to be done."

The conclusion is that the Davis-Bacon requirement did increase the cost of projects outside metropolitan areas. Furthermore, within metropolitan areas where nonunion labor was a viable alternative, the Davis-Bacon requirement also imposed higher construction costs. Ironically, its heaviest impact in raising hospital costs fell on the areas that had been singled out for federal support—small communities. [12]

Construction and renovation grants gave the state Hill-Burton agency a great deal of power to implement its plans. There are reports that hospitals were required to add new services such as emergency rooms or obstetrical services in order to be considered for a Hill-Burton grant. These reports are difficult to verify and it would be even more difficult to estimate their cost implications. One regulation that has proved to be a center of controversy in recent years is the federal requirement that hospitals that have received Hill-Burton grants must provide at least a minimum level of care to patients who cannot pay. The details of the regulation have been changed, but in general the rule requires that 3 to 5 percent of care be free. It is evident that a hospital that had been giving about 1 percent free care and was then forced to give 5 percent would find itself making a free-care contribution larger than the Hill-Burton grant it received.[13]

Conclusion

The data presented in this chapter indicate that federal funds flowed in accordance with the intentions of the Hill-Burton program. More money went to low-income states, and in both low-income states and counties with low median family income, federal monies financed a higher proportion of the cost of a project than elsewhere.

In the early years of the program, short-term hospitals received the greatest benefit. In later years funds were increasingly allocated to other types of facilities, and a very high portion of funds supported modernization. The position of relatively small communities as the major recipients of funds under the program does not seem to have changed very much through 1971. The real value of Hill-Burton funds is less than the $3.7 billion provided, because some of the requirements of the program, in particular the Davis-Bacon requirement, increased the costs of projects.

CHAPTER III

EFFECT OF HILL-BURTON ON REAL RESOURCES

The flow of the grant funds made available through the Hill-Burton program has been in accordance with the intentions of the law. To evaluate the program, however, we must go beyond a simple study of money flow and determine whether the program was effective in achieving its goals.

The goals of the program in 1946 can be loosely separated into two parts: (1) to increase the supply of hospital beds and improve the distribution of medical services, and (2) to rationalize the planning of physical facilities with respect to their location and coordination.

Effect on the General Shortage of Hospital Beds

At the 1940 and 1945 hearings before the subcommittee of the Senate Committee on Education and Labor on the original Hospital Survey and Construction Act, stress was laid on the general shortage of hospital facilities, although estimates of its extent differed. Under the law, Hill-Burton agencies were to take a census of hospital facilities, determine which beds were "conforming," and estimate how many additional beds were needed.[1] These estimates were to form the basis for policy.

According to data published by HEW, in 1948 there were 469,398 short-term hospital beds, 83 percent of which were conforming. The state agencies estimated that about 56 percent more beds were needed. In 1969 there were 826,711 beds (40 percent of which had been partially supported by Hill-Burton funds); 70 percent were considered to be conforming, and about 11 percent more beds were needed, many because of shifts in the geographical distribution of the population.[2]

Data on most of the other types of facilities assisted by Hill-Burton are less meaningful since the standards are arbitrary; the exception is long-term facilities. In 1957, there were 267,356 long-term beds; 58 percent were considered to be conforming and an estimated 285 percent more (including modernization of substandard facilities) were needed. In 1969, there were 772,164 long-term beds (12 percent built with some Hill-Burton support), of which 65 percent were considered conforming; an estimated 22 percent more were needed. These figures refer to beds in skilled nursing homes, where the largest part of the increase over this period took place, to long-term and chronic-care facilities, and to long-term units in hospitals. The number of beds in chronic and long-term care facilities, outside of hospitals and nursing homes, actually fell because of the reduced need for tuberculosis and psychiatric facilities.

According to Hill-Burton data, the general shortage of hospital beds has been largely eliminated. Thus, one of the goals of the program has been met. The program may, however, have been too successful. The current Hill-Burton definition of need is based on current bed use, target rates for hospital occupancy, and projected population growth. To the extent that current bed use is inappropriate, Hill-Burton estimates of need will be incorrect.

Hospital utilization patterns depend upon many factors, including the type of insurance coverage and the costs and availability of alternative medical resources.[3] For example, rates of hospitalization of a population served by a large prepaid group practice are much lower than in insured groups with fee-for-service reimbursement (such as Blue Cross).[4] Some studies suggest that, by medical criteria, a substantial number of patients at any given time do not "need" to be hospitalized.[5] On this evidence, current utilization patterns probably exaggerate current needs and the Hill-Burton agencies therefore have overestimated the number of hospital beds needed. These kinds of studies have led many observers to believe that the nation has a surplus of beds.

Distribution of Short-Term Hospital Beds

One of the basic goals of the Hill-Burton program was to improve the distribution of short-term hospital beds among the states. A principal determinant of the number of beds per capita in the early 1940s seemed to be state per capita income—indeed, the correlation between the two in 1942 was 0.76. The large variation in beds per capita, and the fact that poor states had few beds, seemed to be inequitable and to warrant governmental action.

Hill-Burton grant funds were allocated partly on the basis of per capita income. The sponsors of a project, however, had to meet a large fraction of the total construction cost. To decrease the costs to sponsors in low-income states, the sponsor's share varied directly with the state's per capita income. Because these provisions would increase the availability of capital to hospitals (nonprofit, state, and local) in the low-income states, Congress hoped that they would stimulate a major increase in the number of beds there.

Did the program do so in fact? Did it promote a more nearly equal distribution in the number of beds?

Consider first the basic facts. The total number of hospital beds (long- and short-term) per thousand population decreased from a state average of 9.5 in 1947 to 7.7 in 1970, while the number of short-term beds increased from 3.3 to 4.3.[6] The major factors contributing to the decline in total beds were the lowered incidence of tuberculosis and new methods of treating this disease and mental illness. In 1970 the number of beds per capita was more nearly equal across states than it had been in 1947. The coefficient of variation (a measure of dispersion) of total beds per capita across the states decreased from 0.24 in 1947 to 0.20 in 1970, while the coefficient of variation for short-term beds per capita decreased from 0.24 to 0.19. More important, the correlation between state income per capita and total beds per capita decreased from 0.69 in 1947 to 0.25 in 1970, while the correlation between state income per capita and short-term beds per capita dropped from 0.62 to −0.15. We therefore conclude that the distribution of hospital beds across states has become more nearly equal (although this may have caused greater differences in occupancy ratios). But the question remains: was the Hill-Burton program the cause?

Determinants of the Number of Hospital Beds

Both demand and supply factors influence the number of hospital beds built in a state. The demand for hospitalization is dependent on the age, sex, race, and income mix of the population; the extent of insurance coverage; attitudes toward medical care; and general factors affecting disease level and overall health status. For example, hospitalization rates are higher than average for the very young, the elderly, and women during their child-bearing years. Supply factors include the existence of community organizations (government, churches and other voluntary organizations, and profit-seeking

27

companies) that could build and operate a hospital; the availability of capital from philanthropic funds and government grants; and the prospects for operating revenues.

The Hill-Burton program operates by increasing the supply of capital funds. But while it can provide major resources, it need not change what would have happened in its absence. If grant funds are substituted for other funds (which then are allocated to other activities) or if they support the construction of more luxurious and elaborate hospitals, grants will not increase the number of beds built. This question is one that can be settled only by analyzing the change in hospital beds per capita over time.

Estimating the effect of the program calls for a reliable measure of the extent of Hill-Burton activity in each state. Three possible measures are the number of beds constructed under partial Hill-Burton support, the average support for each such bed, and the proportion of beds existing in 1970 that were partially supported by Hill-Burton. The problem with each of these is that it reflects all the supply and demand factors for hospital beds, rather than the contribution of the Hill-Burton program to the supply.

The Hill-Burton program never paid the entire cost of a project; in general, it covered 20 to 50 percent of the cost; the balance had to come from philanthropy, other government grants, or current revenue, whose availability depended on the demand for hospital services in each community.[7] Thus, the number of hospital beds partially supported by Hill-Burton confuses the effect of the program with the other supply and demand factors in the community. The amount of subsidy per bed and the percentage of 1970 beds supported by Hill-Burton in reality measure how the state Hill-Burton agency decided to allocate its funds. Since states rarely gave individual projects the maximum subsidy permitted under the law, these measures serve more to suggest how thin the state agencies decided to spread the funds than to weigh the effect of the program.

We decided that the best measure was the simple one of the number of Hill-Burton dollars per capita going to each state. This measure isolates the effect of the program from that of other supply factors and from state agency decisions on allocating the funds. In particular, we defined the measure as the total funds allocated to a state between 1947 and 1971 divided by the 1960 population (a measure of the average population in the state over this period).

We found that the various measures mentioned above are correlated and the results of the analysis would be similar no matter which was used. Indeed, the correlation between our measure of the Hill-Burton program and the proportion of beds in each state that as of 1970 had received some Hill-Burton support is 0.72.

In order to estimate the effect of the Hill-Burton program, we should construct a model that specifies explicitly both supply and demand factors. We have not elected to do that for a number of reasons, most notably the limitations of the data. Nonetheless, we believe the models presented should give good estimates of the effect of the program.

Empirical Results: Hospital Beds

Data are available on many of the important supply and demand variables within each state. These are defined and their means and standard deviations shown in Table 8, along with Hill-Burton funds

Table 8

MEANS AND STANDARD DEVIATIONS OF VARIABLES USED IN THE ANALYSIS OF EFFECTS OF HILL-BURTON PROGRAM

Name of Variable	Mean	Standard Deviation
Change Variables [a]		
Short-term beds per 1,000 population [b]	1.368	.325
Total beds per 1,000 population [b]	.844	.180
Proprietary hospitals as percent of short-term hospitals [b]	.365	.343
Proprietary beds as a percent of total short-term beds [b]	.508	.65
State personal income per capita [b]	3.013	.419
Percent of state population in communities over 2,500 [c]	1.215	.168
Percent of population with hospital insurance [c, d]	2.165	.940
State population [b]	1.469	.488
Percent of population over 65 [c]	1.368	.180
Hill-Burton measure [e]	24.68	7.96
Absolute Variables [f]		
Occupancy rate (1970) [g]	76.13	5.30
Number of short-term beds per 1,000 population (1970)	4.30	.81
Average hospital size, in beds (1970)	140.5	63.5
Number of medical doctors per 1,000 population (1950)	1.13	.31
Number of places in medical schools per 100,000 population (1950)	12.64	12.34

29

Table 8 (continued)

Personal income per capita (1950)	1,401	324.6
Total beds per 1,000 population (1950)	9.37	2.21
Percent nonrural (1950)	55.56	16.01
Number of medical doctors per 1,000 population (1970)	1.36	.35
Number of places in medical schools per 100,000 population (1970)	16.35	12.90
Personal income per capita (1970)	3,642	553.6
Total beds per 1,000 population (1970)	7.72	1.58
Percent nonrural (1970)	65.78	14.37

[a] Used in regressions reported in Tables 10, 11, and 15.

[b] 1970 value divided by 1947 value.

[c] 1970 value divided by 1950 value.

[d] All people over 65 were assumed to be covered by insurance in 1970.

[e] Total amount of Hill-Burton funds allocated to state (1947-71) divided by state's 1960 population.

[f] Used in regressions reported in Tables 13 and 14.

[g] Average daily census divided by the average number of beds maintained for use.

Source: Basic hospital data for 1947—"Hospital Guide Issue," *Hospitals*, vol. 22 (1948); for 1950—*Hospitals*, vol. 25 (1951); for 1970—*Hospitals*, vol. 45 (1971). Income data for 1947—Charles F. Schwartz and Robert E. Gorham, "Personal Income by State since 1929," *A Supplement to the Survey of Current Business* (Washington, D. C.: U.S. Government Printing Office, 1956); for 1950 and 1970—U.S. Department of Commerce, *Statistical Abstract of the United States, 1972*, p. 319. Population data for 1947—*Statistical Abstract, 1949*, p. 31; for 1950, 1960, and 1970—*Statistical Abstract, 1972*, p. 12. Insurance data for 1950—Health Insurance Council, *Annual Survey of Accident and Health Coverage in the United States as of December 31, 1951*; for 1970—*Annual Survey of Accident and Health Coverage in the United States as of December 31, 1971*. Data on the elderly for 1950—Federal Security Agency, *Fact Book on Aging* (Washington, D. C.: U.S. Government Printing Office, 1952); for 1970—*Statistical Abstract, 1972*, p. 31. Hill-Burton measure data—U.S. Department of Health, Education and Welfare, *Hill-Burton Project Register*, pp. 23-25. Data on medical doctors for 1950—M. Altenderfer and M. Pennell, *Health Manpower Source Book: Industry and Occupations Data from the 1951 Census*, U.S. Public Health Service, 1954; for 1970—*Statistical Abstract, 1970*. Medical school places for 1950—"Medical Education," *Journal of the American Medical Association*, vol. 147, no. 2 (September 1951), pp. 136-137; for 1970—"Medical Education," *Journal of the American Medical Association*, vol. 214, no. 8 (November 1970), pp. 1488-1489.

per capita. The change variables are measured as the ratio of the 1970 value to the 1947 value. For example, total beds per capita fell an average of 16 percent over this period (due to the fall in long-term beds), since the mean of this variable is 0.84. Making the variables into ratios permits interpreting them as percentage changes over the period.

Table 9 shows that the demographic, socioeconomic, and other variables are highly correlated. This means that any attempt to in-

Table 9

SIMPLE CORRELATIONS BETWEEN CHANGE VARIABLES SHOWN IN TABLES 10, 11, AND 15

Variable	Income per Capita	Percent Urbani- zation	Percent Insur- ance	Percent Elderly	Popu- lation Growth	Hill- Burton Measure	Total Beds per 1,000	Short- Term Beds per 1,000	Percent Proprie- tary Hospitals	Percent Proprie- tary Beds
Income per capita	1.00									
Percent urbanization	.30	1.00								
Percent insurance	.49	.73	1.00							
Percent elderly	.37	.52	.58	1.00						
Population growth	.11	.12	.11	−.11	1.00					
Hill-Burton measure	.46	.58	.71	.42	−.10	1.00				
Total beds per thousand	.51	.13	.26	.47	−.42	.47	1.00			
Short-term beds per thousand	.46	.52	.49	.63	−.49	.51	.60	1.00		
Percent proprietary hospitals	.14	−.02	−.02	.20	.25	−.21	.06	−.11	1.00	
Percent proprietary beds	.03	−.08	−.05	.04	.30	−.25	−.11	−.22	.91	1.00

vestigate the effect of the Hill-Burton program by correlation (or univariate) analysis will produce biased results. Only when all of the factors hypothesized to affect the change in hospital beds per capita are included will the estimated coefficients be interpretable. Including all of the variables, however, will give rise to problems of multicollinearity. Thus, the estimated coefficients will have large standard errors, which appropriately reflect the dispersion of the estimate.

Table 10 reports a series of regressions in which the change from 1947 to 1970 in total beds per thousand population for a state is estimated as a function of the demographic and other variables. The change in short-term beds per capita for a state is similarly analyzed in Table 11.

The first regression in each table has a single explanatory variable, the Hill-Burton funds per capita in the state. Demographic and economic information is added in the second, and the growth rate of the state population in the third. States with the highest rate of population growth would be expected to have a lower rate of increase in hospital beds per capita, since they would have had to build beds rapidly (even without outside support) just to maintain a steady ratio of beds to population. Regression (4) is regression (2) with the addition of a variable characterizing the census region, while regression (5) embodies the same addition to regression (3). Many differences between regions (such as climate or ways of practicing medicine) are not captured by the small number of demographic and economic variables, so the regional dummy variables are included to account for the possibility that these missing variables may be correlated with the Hill-Burton measure and produce a biased estimate. For example, because the South had few beds per capita in 1947 and had a low income per capita it received large sums through the Hill-Burton program. At the same time, it tended to develop more rapidly than other parts of the country, with consequent increases in per capita income and government expenditures. The dummy variable helps to distinguish the effects of few beds in 1947 and the rapid increase in income and government expenditures from that of the Hill-Burton program.

The first regression in each table shows a significant association between Hill-Burton funds per capita and the increase in hospital beds per thousand population. As the additional variables are added, the estimated effect of the Hill-Burton program remains consistent and statistically significant for the case of total hospital beds. The relationship is somewhat more equivocal for short-term hospital

Table 10

FACTORS AFFECTING THE 1947–70 CHANGE IN TOTAL HOSPITAL BEDS PER THOUSAND [a]

Independent Variable	Regression Number				
	(1)	(2)	(3)	(4)	(5)
Constant term	.5835 (7.65)	-.0144 (-.06)	.1918 (.79)	.5713 (1.90)	.5977 (1.90)
Personal income per capita [b]	—	.1530 (2.77)	.1393 (2.93)	.0263 (.40)	.0259 (.39)
Percent nonrural [c]	—	-.2498 (-1.43)	-.2041 (-1.22)	-.4859 (-2.43)	-.4751 (-2.31)
Percent population with hospital insurance [c]	—	-.0705 (-1.84)	-.0496 (-1.32)	-.0240 (-.71)	-.0214 (-.61)
Percent population over 65 [c]	—	.4581 (3.35)	.3920 (2.93)	.3782 (3.12)	.3675 (2.89)
Percent population growth [b]	—	—	-.0930 (-2.26)	—	-.0149 (-.83)
Hill-Burton measure	.0105 (3.58)	.0115 (3.20)	.0096 (2.71)	.0131 (3.72)	.0126 (3.33)
Northeast [d]	—	—	—	-.0884	-.0879
Middle Atlantic	—	—	—	-.0286	-.0304
South Atlantic	—	—	—	.0488	.0540

Table 10 (continued)

Independent Variable	Regression Number				
	(1)	(2)	(3)	(4)	(5)
East North Central	—	—	—	.0437	.0418
East South Central	—	—	—	.1354	.1327
West North Central	—	—	—	.1025	.0979
West South Central	—	—	—	.0129	.0122
Mountain	—	—	—	−.1785	−.1711
Pacific	—	—	—	−.0479	−.0488
R^2 adjusted	.201	.443	.495	.625	.618

[a] The numbers in parentheses are t-statistics.
[b] 1970 value divided by 1947 value.
[c] 1970 value divided by 1950 value.
[d] In these and subsequent regressions involving regional dummy variables, the results are reported so that the sum of all regions is zero.

Table 11

FACTORS AFFECTING THE 1947–70 CHANGE IN SHORT-TERM BEDS PER THOUSAND[a]

Independent Variable	Regression Number				
	(1)	(2)	(3)	(4)	(5)
Constant term	.8584 (6.39)	-.8326 (-1.95)	-.1505 (-.41)	-.5017 (-1.04)	-.2100 (-.45)
Personal income per capita[b]	—	.1743 (1.78)	.1292 (1.66)	.1188 (1.13)	.1151 (1.18)
Percent nonrural[c]	—	.5010 (1.62)	.6520 (2.64)	.2092 (.65)	.3287 (1.09)
Percent population with hospital insurance[c]	—	-.0825 (-1.22)	-.0134 (-.24)	-.0626 (-1.15)	-.0340 (-.66)
Percent population over 65[c]	—	.8098 (3.34)	.5913 (3.01)	.9088 (4.67)	.7907 (4.23)
Population[b]	—	—	-.3077 (-5.09)	—	-.1643 (-2.51)
Hill-Burton measure	.0208 (3.99)	.0096 (1.52)	.0033 (.64)	.0147 (2.61)	.0099 (1.77)
Northeast	—	—	—	-.0697	-.0649
Middle Atlantic	—	—	—	-.0928	-.1132
South Atlantic	—	—	—	-.2537	-.1970

Table 11 (*continued*)

Independent Variable	Regression Number				
	(1)	(2)	(3)	(4)	(5)
East North Central	—	—	—	.1763	.1557
East South Central	—	—	—	.1484	.1181
West North Central	—	—	—	.1432	.0917
West South Central	—	—	—	.1092	.1008
Mountain	—	—	—	−.2308	−.1504
Pacific	—	—	—	.0697	.0592
R^2 adjusted	.241	.466	.665	.707	.746

a The numbers in parentheses are *t*-statistics.
b 1970 value divided by 1947 value.
c 1970 value divided by 1950 value.

beds, although it appears that the Hill-Burton program did finance an increase in the ratio between short-term beds and population.

States in which income per capita rose most rapidly built more hospital beds, both long- and short-term, although this effect becomes fuzzy when the regional dummy variables are added. States in which the rate of urbanization was faster tended to build fewer long-term beds and more short-term beds. Differences in the increase in hospital insurance apparently are not very important. An increase in the proportion of older people in the population led states to build more hospital beds, both long- and short-term. This effect was an extremely significant one. Finally, the states with the greatest growth in population had the smallest growth in beds per capita, although the effect was statistically significant only for short-term beds.

The regional dummy variables show that, other things held constant, the Northeast had a relative decline of about 9 percent in total hospital beds per capita. The East South Central and West North Central had increases of about 15 percent and 11 percent respectively. The Mountain states had a decline of about 19 percent. The decline for the Northeast might be expected, since this region had many more beds per capita in the initial period. The tremendous increases in the East South Central and West North Central probably came about both because these areas were underbedded initially, and because of the rapid increases in income. There doesn't seem to be any easy explanation for the tremendous decline for the Mountain states. In Table 11, the dummy variables indicate much more disparity in the change in short-term beds per capita. For example, the South Atlantic and Mountain states had declines on the order of 21 percent. The East North Central, East South Central, West North Central, and West South Central all had substantial increases, ranging up to about 15 percent. It is evident that there were substantial variations in the change in short-term beds per capita, across different regions, from 1947 to 1970. However, the reasons for these variations among regions are not entirely clear.

The regressions were successful in that they explained over half of the variance in the growth of beds per capita. The last regression explained 61 percent of the variation in the change in total beds per thousand and 74.6 percent of the variation in the change in short-term beds per thousand.

The regressions indicate that the Hill-Burton program had a generally significant effect on the change in hospital beds per capita between 1947 and 1970. For a state that had the average level of support ($24 per person) and the average number of beds per thousand in 1947 (3.1 short-term beds), the estimated cost of an extra bed per thousand was an increase in the Hill-Burton subsidy of $33,000 per thousand population. According to these estimates, the Hill-Burton subsidy of $24 per capita financed slightly less than one additional bed per thousand people over this period.[8]

The average cost of building a hospital bed over these years was a good deal less than $33,000. For construction in general hospitals supported by Hill-Burton, the average cost per bed was $27,000, of which Hill-Burton paid $7,700. The average cost per bed in any type of facility covered by the program was $24,000, of which Hill-Burton paid $7,000. The cost of constructing a bed in a new hospital was less than $27,000. The reason beds supported by Hill-Burton tended to be more expensive was the extensive support the program gave for improvement of ancillary services and other activities that did not affect the number of beds.

Effect on Occupancy Rates

Were the beds financed by the Hill-Burton program used? Their simple existence does not guarantee that they were. Hospital beds are but one medical input, for which ambulatory care can be substituted, at least in part. They can stand empty, or be used in a way that increases costs without bringing about a commensurate improvement in the quality of care.

The answer to the question begins with a comparison of the average occupancy rates in hospitals supported by the program with that for all hospitals, controlling for hospital size (see Table 12).[9] This rate, which is equal to the ratio of the average daily census to the average number of beds maintained during the twelve-month reporting period, measures how intensively a hospital's capacity is used. The 1970 average occupancy rates in hospitals supported by Hill-Burton compared favorably with those for all nonprofit hospitals. The occupancy rates in Hill-Burton-supported hospitals were slightly lower than those of proprietary hospitals when only very small hospitals (six to fifty beds) are considered and slightly higher than proprietary hospitals when hospitals with more than fifty beds are considered. Thus, these data do not suggest that the Hill-Burton program contributed to excess capacity.

While Hill-Burton occupancy rates compare favorably with others of the same size, the rates for *all* hospitals with less than 200 beds are very low. These hospitals are not quite three-quarters full, and the very small ones remain half empty most of the time. This has special impact on overall Hill-Burton rates, because, consistent

Table 12

AVERAGE OCCUPANCY, SELECTED SIZES AND TYPES OF HOSPITALS, 1970
(in percents)

Hospital Size (beds)	Hill-Burton Sample	Non-government, Nonprofit	Proprietary	All Short-Term Hospitals[a] except Federal and Proprietary
6– 24	59.2	52.8	63.7	54.0
25– 49	65.9	63.0	67.0	62.8
50– 99	72.9	72.0	71.4	70.7
100–199	77.1	76.9	74.0	76.1
200–299	79.8	81.1	78.7	80.5
300–399	81.6	83.3	78.4	82.4
400–499	84.6	85.2	—	79.9
500 and over	80.6	84.8	—	82.4

[a] These are hospitals eligible for Hill-Burton support.
Source: "Hospital Guide Issue," *Hospitals,* 1 August 1971, p. 464.

with the rural bias originally built into the program, the average size of the hospitals it supported was small. The 1970 sizes of the hospitals in the one-fifth sample bear out this observation: [10]

Size of hospitals (beds)	Number of hospitals
6-24	12
25-49	102
50-99	133
100-199	135
200-299	79
300-399	40
400-499	16
500 and over	31

The comparison set out in Table 12 neglects the possibility that the new beds attracted physicians and patients at the expense of nearby hospitals with older plants. This possibility can be examined by analyzing the factors that affect the occupancy rate, including a measure of the Hill-Burton subsidy. As shown in Table 13, our analysis attempts to explain the average occupancy rate in a state's short-term hospitals by the number of short-term beds per capita, the average size of its hospitals, its Hill-Burton funds per capita from 1947 to 1971, and variables for the ten census regions.

The first regression shows that more Hill-Burton support decreases occupancy, although the effect is not statistically significant. As the second regression makes clear, the association of the Hill-Burton measure with lower occupancy rates is due to the small average size of hospitals in the states that received substantial Hill-Burton funds. Regression (2) indicates that, as one might expect, occupancy rates are lower in states with the most beds per capita and in states with the smallest hospitals. States receiving the most Hill-Burton funds had the highest occupancy rates, controlling for beds per capita and hospital size.

Table 13

FACTORS AFFECTING THE AVERAGE HOSPITAL OCCUPANCY RATE, 1970[a]

Independent Variable	Regression Number		
	(1)	(2)	(3)
Constant term	80.19 (32.52)	64.44 (14.90)	72.63 (18.12)
Short-term beds per thousand	—	−1.11 (−1.93)	−1.89 (−2.70)
Average size of hospitals (beds)	—	.08 (7.91)	.04 (3.68)
Hill-Burton measure	−.16 (−1.73)	.24 (3.19)	.03 (.28)
Northeast	—	—	50.33
Middle Atlantic	—	—	−3.78
South Atlantic	—	—	−4.71
East North Central	—	—	−5.42
East South Central	—	—	−1.98
West North Central	—	—	−6.04
West South Central	—	—	−7.08
Mountain	—	—	−9.98
Pacific	—	—	−11.37
R^2 adjusted	.041	.663	.771

[a] The numbers in parentheses are t-statistics.

Not much sense can be made of the Hill-Burton coefficient, however, since regression (3) (which adds the dummy variables for region) has an estimated coefficient that is unimportant in terms of either policy or significance. Thus, the regressions indicate that the average occupancy rate of hospitals in a state is negatively related to the number of beds per capita and positively related to the average size of hospitals. These occupancy rates are much higher in the Northeast and somewhat lower in other regions, particularly in the Pacific. (If the Northeast serves as a referral area for other parts of the nation, such a pattern would be expected, along with higher than expected beds per capita in this region.)

Occupancy rates tell us about current utilization patterns, but not about which hospital admissions were necessary and certainly not whether an additional hospital bed was necessary. There is evidence that additional beds do have a minor effect in producing lower occupancy rates.

Effect of Hill-Burton on Distribution of Doctors

The sponsors of the Hill-Burton program believed that if they could encourage the building of hospital beds in areas where there were relatively few medical resources, they would attract physicians to those areas. Dr. Thomas Parran, then surgeon general of the United States Public Health Service, stated at the 1945 House hearings, "The presence of hospital and diagnostic facilities, possibly more than any other factor, determines the distribution and professional skill of physicians." [11]

How do hospital beds in fact affect the distribution of physicians? A series of studies has investigated the factors affecting the distribution of physicians across states, including expected income, interaction with colleagues, training facilities, and the quality of life associated with living and working in a particular area. Unfortunately, with the exception of the work by Fuchs and Kramer, who found a significant effect,[12] hospital beds and other support facilities have not been used as explanatory variables in regressions where the state has been the unit of analysis. In analyses within a state or within metropolitan areas that have included the number of hospital beds or their proximity, they have been significant. Kaplan and Leinhardt found, for example, that proximity to colleagues and access to hospitals were the crucial factors in the decisions of urban physicians about office location.[13] All of the analyses have identified the availability of medical training facilities as important to the location of physicians.[14] By building on previous analyses, we will try to account for the variation in the number of medical doctors per 1,000 population across the states.

We hypothesize that the number of physicians per thousand population in a state depends on the number of hospital beds per thousand, personal income per capita, the number of medical school places per 100,000 population, and the proportion of the population living in urban areas. We did not have measures of other important variables, such as licensing restrictions and physician incomes. We accepted Dr. Parran's conjecture, and hypothesized that states with more hospital beds would have more physicians.

As shown in Table 14, a regression of physicians per thousand population on these factors supported our hypotheses. Hospital

Table 14

FACTORS AFFECTING THE DISTRIBUTION OF DOCTORS PER THOUSAND POPULATION, 1950 AND 1970 [a]

Independent Variable	1950 Regression number (1)	(2)	1970 Regression number (3)	(4)
Constant term	−.1470 (−1.54)	−.0967 (−.60)	−.6239 (−2.60)	.0234 (.08)
Total beds per thousand	.0446 (3.78)	.0316 (2.36)	.0425 (1.81)	.0374 (1.56)
Personal income per capita	.0001 (1.07)	.0001 (1.18)	.0003 (2.72)	.0001 (1.26)
Training places per 100,000	.0057 (3.52)	.0068 (3.95)	.0076 (3.03)	.0102 (4.96)
Percent nonrural	.0113 (6.32)	.0118 (5.44)	.0084 (2.27)	.0103 (3.32)
Northeast	—	.3334	—	.2840
Middle Atlantic	—	.0322	—	.1466
South Atlantic	—	−.0059	—	−.0117
East North Central	—	−.1883	—	−.1864
East South Central	—	−.0880	—	−.1816
West North Central	—	.0190	—	−.1416
West South Central	—	−.0737	—	−.1865
Mountain	—	−.0173	—	.0583
Pacific	—	−.0126	—	.2233
R^2 adjusted	.821	.831	.620	.775

[a] The numbers in parentheses are t-statistics.

beds were a statistically significant factor in attracting physicians, as were the number of places in medical schools and the proportion of the population living in urban areas. Furthermore, these relationships held true for both 1950 and 1970.[15] When short-term beds per capita were substituted for total beds (in unreported regressions), the explanatory power of the regression rose in 1950, though not in 1970. Personal income per capita was generally not important in attracting physicians.

We conclude that the Hill-Burton program probably has affected the distribution of physicians. It promoted an increase in total hospital beds per capita, and these beds have a statistically significant attraction for physicians.

This analysis does not study the success of the program in attracting physicians to rural areas. That question requires an analysis of the number of physicians per capita by community size along with data on the presence of a hospital in the community. It is interesting to note, however, that in 1971 there were 133 counties that did not have a physician and 599 counties without a hospital. But there were only 5 counties that had a hospital but no physician. Available evidence suggests that physicians are more likely—but not necessarily—to locate where there are hospital beds.

Changed Ownership Structure of Hospitals

The nonprofit hospitals—voluntary and public hospitals—have been the recipients of Hill-Burton grant funds. While the controversy on the relative merits of voluntary and proprietary hospitals has no place in this report, the comparisons that follow serve to highlight three general issues. The first is construction costs, the second is the degree of freedom and pluralism in the overall system, and the third is the relative ability of the two types of hospitals to adjust to changing conditions.

First, because all hospitals have become more elaborate and luxurious since 1947, the possibility that the Hill-Burton program has resulted in more elaborate and luxurious hospitals is difficult to verify directly.[16] Some evidence came in the 1970 Senate hearings, which produced a dramatic comparison of voluntary and proprietary hospitals. A study comparing the construction costs of the two types of hospitals revealed that a 100-bed voluntary hospital cost three times as much as a like proprietary hospital—$3,352,700 compared with $1,137,000.[17] This disparity reflects an enormous difference in the facilities and services offered. And it raises important questions: Doesn't such a large difference suggest that the expenditures for the voluntary hospital are excessive? Given the lively concern over reducing the cost of hospital care, wouldn't the public be better off with more proprietary hospitals or with less elaborate voluntary hospitals?

Second, the medical-care delivery system in the United States is a pluralistic one, vastly diverse in organization and in method. The resulting competition of ideas, incentives to innovate, and rewards for satisfying public desires have been highly beneficial. We would be loath to see this diversity lost through explicit government attempts to subsidize one idea over others. Instead of prescribing the *organization* of delivery—by, say, favoring health maintenance organizations or voluntary hospitals—the government should be pursuing *goals*—say, promoting the best health status of the population for a given expenditure. If some organizational form provides care that is too expensive or of poor quality, it is the results and the incentive producing these results that should be condemned, not the organizational form.

On the third issue, Steinwald and Neuhauser argue that proprietary hospitals are more adaptable to change than are voluntary ones.[18] This argument is plausible since entrepreneurs typically adjust to changing conditions more rapidly than nonprofit organizations, which are more isolated from market conditions. But the assertion must be tested.

These three arguments have been raised here because the Hill-Burton program excluded proprietary hospitals from government grants. In view of the substantial subsidies given to the nonprofit sector since 1946, this exclusion should have hurt proprietary hospitals. Indeed, in 1947 about 21 percent of short-term hospitals were proprietary, as were 10 percent of the beds; but by 1970 the proportions were only about 9 percent and 5 percent, respectively. Was the Hill-Burton program responsible for this change?

To answer this question we have collected data on the factors that are expected to affect the growth of proprietary hospitals and beds (those that were used to examine the growth of all hospital beds). The percentage changes in the proportion of proprietary short-term hospitals and beds are regressed on these variables, with the results that are presented in Table 15. The regressions explain only a small percentage of the decline in market share of the proprietary beds. The market share declined less where the growth rate of the population was highest and where the proportion of the population over 65 rose most rapidly, a result consistent with the hypothesis that the proprietaries are more adaptable. The effect of

Table 15

FACTORS AFFECTING THE CHANGE IN THE RELATIVE IMPORTANCE OF PROPRIETARY HOSPITALS, 1947–70[a]

Independent Variable	Proprietary Hospitals					Proprietary Beds		
	Regression number					Regression number		
	(1)	(2)	(3)	(4)	(5)	(6)	(7)	(8)
Constant term	.590 (3.66)	−4.834 (−.82)	−.9565 (−1.56)	−.0106 (−1.66)	1.014 (3.36)	.2783 (.24)	−.6469 (−.54)	−.1321 (−1.18)
Personal income per capita [b]	—	.1936 (1.43)	.2248 (1.71)	.1696 (1.26)	—	.1923 (.72)	.2534 (.98)	.2215 (.94)
Percent nonrural [c]	—	.0540 (.13)	−.0507 (−.12)	.3396 (.81)	—	−.1016 (−.12)	−.3064 (−.37)	.4527 (.62)
Percent population with hospital insurance [c]	—	−.0008 (−.01)	−.0488 (−.52)	−.1169 (−1.64)	—	.1201 (.65)	.0264 (.14)	−.1296 (−1.04)
Percent population over 65 [c]	—	.5509 (1.64)	.7025 (2.12)	.4344 (1.69)	—	.3494 (.53)	.6458 (.99)	.1736 (.39)
Population growth [b]	—	—	.2134 (2.10)	.2795 (3.09)	—	—	.4173 (2.09)	.6222 (3.94)
Hill-Burton measure	−.009 (−1.47)	−.1964 (−2.23)	−.0153 (−1.75)	.0017 (.23)	−.020 (−1.75)	−.0373 (−2.15)	−.0287 (−1.67)	.0048 (.36)
Northeast	—	—	—	−.1926	—	—	—	−.1218
Middle Atlantic	—	—	—	.8349	—	—	—	.3904
South Atlantic	—	—	—	−.1672	—	—	—	−.3042

Table 15 (continued)

Independent Variable	Proprietary Hospitals				Proprietary Beds			
	(1)	Regression number (2)	(3)	(4)	(5)	Regression number (6)	(7)	(8)
East North Central	—	—	—	−.1303	—	—	—	−.2093
East South Central	—	—	—	−.0642	—	—	—	.0611
West North Central	—	—	—	−.2192	—	—	—	−.0987
West South Central	—	—	—	−.0004	—	—	—	−.1629
Mountain	—	—	—	−.2212	—	—	—	−.2546
Pacific	—	—	—	−.1602	—	—	—	−.3745
R^2 adjusted	.0241	.088	.156	.572	.0421	.009	.082	.633

a The numbers in parentheses are t-statistics.
b 1970 value divided by 1947 value.
c 1970 value divided by 1950 value.

46

the Hill-Burton program is somewhat equivocal. In six out of eight cases, the regression indicates that the Hill-Burton program was associated with a shrinkage in the market share in proprietary hospitals. In the other two cases, the evidence suggests no association. We conclude that the Hill-Burton program probably caused a decline in the relative importance of proprietary hospitals, but the effect was not important.

Summary and Conclusions

Over the time that the Hill-Burton program functioned, the relative availability of hospital facilities tended to become equalized among the states. The simple relationship between number of beds per capita and state personal income per capita that was so strikingly positive in the early forties disappeared; indeed, the reverse is now true for short-term hospitals. The Hill-Burton program was a factor in achieving these goals. The regression analysis indicated that the program did serve to increase the number of both short-term beds and total beds per thousand, an effect that would not have taken place to the extent it did in the program's absence.

The impact was perhaps not as strong as might have been expected. Occasionally, the Hill-Burton program acted simply as an alternative source of funds for projects that would have been undertaken in any case. It may have enhanced a project through support services, rather than through a net increase in beds.

We did not find evidence that, across the states, the program had a tendency to lower occupancy rates. This does not mean that the additional beds were "needed," but only that those that were built were used (on average, although individual decisions occasionally resulted in unused beds). Since many of the hospitals aided were small and since occupancy rates of such hospitals are characteristically quite low, there is a tendency to conclude that the Hill-Burton program lowered occupancy rates.

We uncovered some slight evidence that the Hill-Burton program contributed to the decline in the share of the proprietary hospitals. We also found that because the Hill-Burton program spurred a net increase in beds, it probably affected the distribution of physicians. Beyond this, by serving to increase the ratio of beds to population, Hill-Burton also contributed to a decrease in the occupancy rate.

CHAPTER IV

METHODS FOR FINANCING AND CONTROLLING HOSPITAL CAPITAL EXPENDITURES

The medical world of 1974 is radically different from that of 1946. There are more short-term beds per capita, and improvements in medical knowledge and the increasing sophistication of equipment have pushed the cost of medical facilities considerably higher. Moreover, the sources of hospital revenues have changed. Instead of primarily serving self-paying and indigent patients, hospitals now provide care mostly to patients whose bills are paid by third parties—Blue Cross, commercial insurance companies, or the government through the Medicare and Medicaid programs. Consequently, while hospital administrators may have great difficulty in financing capital expenditures, they have little in covering operating costs (neglecting the effects of price controls).

This paradox is the hallmark of the current environment. Capital expenditures loom as a much greater concern to hospital administrators and boards than current expenses. The ability to expand or modernize is inextricably tied to reimbursement formulas, and a solution to the problem of financing capital expenditures necessarily involves the complex ways in which a hospital gets its revenue from current operations.

In this chapter we explore these and related issues, such as the interaction between planning agencies and hospital reimbursement.

Capital Expenditures

Much work has been done on both descriptive and normative models of capital financing for profit-making corporations. A profit-making corporation should evaluate a proposed capital expenditure by looking at its implications for future costs and revenues. It should be undertaken only if it appears profitable—that is, only if the discounted surplus of total revenue over total costs with the investment (compared with the case without the investment) is greater than zero. The theory is more complicated than this simple statement implies. Crucial variables to be considered include the cost of capital, the alternative investment possibilities, the amount of risk, and the availability of both equity and debt financing.

While profit maximization is not the goal of most hospitals (since they are nonprofit), sound management practices require similar procedures for evaluation and decision. The cost of expansion or modernization ultimately must be borne by three sources: philanthropy, government, and patient revenues. Philanthropy and government grants are sources of only a small portion of funds. A voluntary hospital with a large mortgage must operate in a businesslike fashion to ensure that its patient revenues will cover interest and principal on borrowed capital (either through accumulated earnings or through payment of interest and depreciation from future earnings). While this is a simplistic statement of the problem, it serves to stress the fact that capital financing is directly related to reimbursement policies.

Current Reimbursement Formulas and Capital Financing

In 1969 about 26.1 percent of the capital expenditures of all short-term hospitals were financed by government, 15.1 percent by philanthropy, 20.1 percent through hospital reserves, and 35 percent by borrowing.[1] The extent to which hospitals can finance capital expenditures through borrowing, or indeed through accumulated reserves, will depend upon two factors: (1) the reimbursement policies of third-party agencies, and (2) the price elasticity of demand for patients who face charges.

Consider a representative hospital in Western Pennsylvania that is contemplating a $10 million modernization program. The hospital is assumed to be breaking even. More than 50 percent of its revenue is received from Blue Cross, Medicare, and Medicaid (see Table 16). The reimbursement formulas developed by the agencies are based on incurred costs which exclude some kinds of costs (such as bad debts).

Now assume that a $10 million modernization program financed by a 6 percent loan and 25-year mortgage has been completed. Hospital costs have now increased by about $300,000 a year in interest and $400,000 per year in amortization. All other costs remain unchanged.[2] What now happens to the hospital's revenue?

Table 16

REVENUE SOURCES AND COSTS OF HYPOTHETICAL HOSPITAL BEFORE AND AFTER $10 MILLION MODERNIZATION

(thousands of dollars)

| | | After Modernization | |
Budget Item	Before Modernization (1)	Without Hill-Burton (2)	With Hill-Burton (3)
Revenue sources			
Blue Cross	2,472	2,596	2,583
Medicare	1,200	1,338	1,332
Medicaid	900	1,004	999
Commercial insurance	1,260		
Self-pay	315	1,673	1,673
Bad debt	(75)		
Total	6,072	6,611	6,588
Costs			
Patient care	6,000	6,000	6,000
Interest	0	300	270
Amortization	72	472	432
Total	6,072	6,772	6,702
Operating deficit	0	161	114

Blue Cross of Western Pennsylvania would pay its portion of the interest costs as long as the total cost per patient-day did not exceed 10 percent more than the mean cost per patient-day of all hospitals in the relevant reimbursement group.[3] Toward amortization, Blue Cross would add to its present payment of $72,000 only an additional $3,600 (calculated as 3 percent of the additional Blue Cross reimbursable cost). Medicare and Medicaid would pay their portions of the interest and amortization. Assume that the hospital can raise its charges to commercially insured and self-pay patients by 11.5 percent (700/6072) without losing any patient-days. Then the revenue and costs after modernization would be as shown in column (2) of Table 16.

These assumptions are generous, giving rise to a financial outcome that is probably better than that which would actually occur. If demand for hospital care on the part of self-pay patients is related to price, then more patients may seek care elsewhere or decide not to be hospitalized. Suppose that the price elasticity is −0.5; then revenue from self-pay and commercially insured patients would increase by only $86,477 (instead of the $172,955 increase that results from a price elasticity of zero). Suppose further that the hospital's average reimbursable costs were at the group mean (say, $100) before the modernization program and that interest would raise those costs to $115; then Blue Cross would pay only two-thirds of the interest charge. Under these circumstances the deficit would be $289,026 per year.

The hospital can hardly expect philanthropy to cover a deficit of $161,349 to $289,026 each year for twenty-five years. Under these circumstances, the hospital cannot afford this modernization program. Indeed, the only feasible modernization is one that is small enough so that the sum of philanthropic contributions and additional revenue from self-pay and commercially insured patients covers the amortization and interest charge that Blue Cross will not.

The role of a Hill-Burton grant in such circumstances is novel. If Hill-Burton gave the hospital a $1 million modernization grant, the annual interest charge would decrease to $270,000 and the amortization charge to $360,000. Assuming that the initial conditions were the same as before, and that Medicare and Medicaid continued to pay their share of interest and depreciation, the revenue and cost would be those reported in column (3) of Table 16.

The $1 million Hill-Burton grant reduces the operating deficit from $161,349 to $114,085. Its impact comes both from the $1 million lower modernization costs and from the maintenance of the Medicare and Medicaid payments on the depreciation on the full $10 million program. However, even the grant is not sufficient to allow the hospital to finance the modernization without philanthropy or increased subsidization from the self-pay patients.

The choice of a Western Pennsylvania hospital was deliberate since Blue Cross of Western Pennsylvania does not pay depreciation. Some Blue Cross plans do pay depreciation, while others pay on the basis of charges. If the depreciation cost is covered by Blue Cross, the main factor to be considered in undertaking the modernization program will be the demand elasticity for self-pay (and commercially insured) patients.

Loan Guarantees

In the last several years, the Hill-Burton program has begun to emphasize guaranteed loans rather than grants to support construction. The model displayed in Table 16 can be used to show that the guaranteed loan may not help a hospital. The program subsidizes the interest rate, as well as guaranteeing the loan. Reducing the interest rate to the hospital reduces the interest charge, but does not affect amortization. This means that charges for self-pay patients and the cost per patient-day need not rise so much (so that the hospital need not incur costs above its ceiling). The principal problem noted above, however, was with financing the amortization rather than interest charges.

Possibly the only justification for such loans would be the unwillingness of the private capital market to lend money for hospital construction. We see no evidence of this. On the contrary, insurance companies and banks seem willing to provide funds for hospital construction as long as careful financial analysis indicates that they can be repaid at the market interest rate.

If this observation is correct, federal guarantees have only three justifications. Two involve the policy makers' motivations; one concerns those of hospitals.

The first is that the government wishes to subsidize hospital construction. For a $10 million project financed by a twenty-five-year mortgage, a reduction of 2 percent in the interest rate is equal to a subsidy of about $100,000 per year, or roughly $1,160,000 (assuming a discount rate of 7 percent). This amounts to about an 11 percent subsidy of the project, spread over twenty-five years rather than donated in an initial lump. Because some third parties pay interest but not depreciation, the hospital benefits more from $1 in a construction grant than in an interest subsidy.

The second reason for guaranteed loans is that they are a way to shift the main burden of the subsidy to future administrations. However politically astute this may be, it amounts to shirking the responsibility for the program. To charge future administrations in an effort to reduce current governmental costs is fiscally irresponsible when no other reason supports a change in policy.

The third reason for guaranteed loans is that they make Uncle Sam co-signer. If the hospital defaults, the government must pay the interest and amortization. But the scheme raises troublesome questions: Are there administrators and boards who, in planning expansions, believe that the future will take care of itself? Do planning agencies forecast demand for hospitalization for the next twenty-five years accurately enough to guarantee that the hospital can meet its commitments? Might not some hospitals undertake an expansion—even though they cannot see where the principal and interest will come from—because the government is co-signer of the mortgage? What will HEW do when a hospital cannot meet payments under a guaranteed loan? Since HEW is unlikely to take over the hospital, or even to force management changes, the hospital faces no costs in defaulting. We forecast that the federal government will find these loans more costly than expected due to the inability of hospitals to cover interest and depreciation. Since guaranteed loans provide the wrong set of incentives to hospitals, they should be abandoned.

Proposals to Reform Reimbursement Formulas

The example given above highlights again the paradox of the voluntary hospitals: they often can cover operating expenses while they are unable to cover the costs of expansion or modernization. Since the annual requirements for expansion and modernization are currently about $1.5 billion, there is little hope that philanthropy or government can be the sole or even principal source of funds. There is no alternative to reforming the reimbursement formulas.

Full-Cost Reimbursement Plus Planning. Because most reimbursement is on a "cost-plus" basis (since it comes from Blue Cross, Medicare, and Medicaid), extending this concept to the financing of capital expenditures is a logical idea. Indeed, Medicare already pays its share of capital costs, as does Medicaid generally and even some Blue Cross plans. But what is the consequence of guaranteeing a hospital that about 80 percent of its total capital and current costs will be automatically covered, as they would be if Blue Cross, Medicare, and Medicaid included full depreciation and interest costs in the rate base? Hospital administrators would have little reason to resist pressure from physicians and others to buy new, specialized, and perhaps underutilized equipment. The increase in costs would be astronomical. Indeed, many observers of the hospital industry believe that third-party financing with formulas based on incurred cost is one of the primary causes of the current inflation in hospital costs.[4]

Many knowledgeable observers have foreseen this cost inflation and have proposed ways to prevent it. One is that planning agencies review hospital capital expenditures.[5] But hospital planners agree neither on the mission of such agencies nor on the criteria for evaluating their performance. For example:

> Areawide hospital planning will probably be judged in two contrasting ways: by those who saw it as a new and creative voluntary process in a health care system characterized by narrow interests and fragmentation, a transition process which set the stage for an even more dynamic health planning activity; and by those who will assess it as a failure, a self-serving mechanism protecting the status quo and

thus destined for extinction. In the latter perspective, perhaps it may be that the failure was not in the areawide endeavor but in the failure of community itself—a reckoning still to come in American society.[6]

The key to the current hospital planning system is the Comprehensive Health Planning B Agency, or Areawide Planning Agency.[7] Each B agency covers a region consisting of a number of counties. It derives its power from the ability to channel federal grants or loan guarantees to shape the hospital plans in its region. In addition, these agencies now have the power to deny reimbursement for care given to patients covered by federal programs if the hospital undertakes capital expenditures in excess of $100,000 without their approval. These agencies will have an even larger role as an increasing number of states adopt legislation concerning certificates of need. This legislation requires the hospital to obtain approval for any capital expenditure over some minimum amount, which has been set as low as $10,000. It would permit the B agency to control capital expenditures and to stop unnecessary building and duplication of facilities. But it would also permit it to stifle innovation, to deny hospital facilities to new communities, and generally to serve the interests of existing hospitals, particular segments of the community, or other special-interest groups.

When the B agencies were initiated, there was an overwhelming concern for consumer participation in solving the problems of medical-care delivery. To achieve it, a requirement was laid down that more than half of each agency's board should consist of "consumers," people with no affiliation to health-care delivery, education, or research. In this way, the argument runs, B agencies will not be subject to the criticism other regulatory agencies have faced: the consumer majority can be expected to prevent the board and thus the agency from catering exclusively to the needs of existing hospitals and medical professionals.

Whatever its other advantages, however, this kind of membership on the board compounds the problem of forecasting the needs of the community and planning to meet them. Consumers cannot be expected to have sufficient knowledge to do this job well or even to appreciate whether the staff of the agency has done it well. Since the predominant role of the agency will very likely be to deny the requests of health-care institutions, the predominance of consumers on the board is apt to mean that the agency will not take as strong stands—or take them as often—as it should. Furthermore, in spite of the move to increase consumer participation, there are yet no models about how consumers should or do participate, nor are health-care professionals trained to interact with consumers. Any board member would require a great deal of knowledge and confidence to deny a facility where enormous political and community pressure is exerted for it. We doubt that any agency—whatever its composition—could resist this pressure. The prospect seems even more doubtful with a preponderance of consumers in control.

The effectiveness of the planning agencies in controlling the level and distribution of capital expenditures will depend on a number of factors.

One is the type of constraint placed on the agencies. If they are enjoined simply to exercise good judgment, they are very likely to respond to the continual pressure from hospitals by approving far too much capital expansion. But, though this sort of constraint is too indefinite, any absolute constraint is likely to be arbitrary, hard to justify, and thus difficult to adhere to.

Another factor is the ability of the planning agency to judge what capital expenditures are needed to increase public welfare. Some people rely on the planning agencies for a wisdom they do not possess. Each hospital can be expected to argue for its viewpoint, and each community to insist on improvements in its hospital. These decisions are troublesome to begin with, and, under pressure, a planning agency will be hard put to develop a base plan or to stick with it.

The history of regulatory agencies in this country suggests that they have not in fact had adequate foresight and that they have not been able to maintain positions against the desires of the regulated.[8] The hospital planning agencies have provided no exception to this observation. We predict that the B agencies will be no more successful in their new role of denying reimbursement under federal programs. We also predict that they will grant too many certificates of need and will generally permit increasing expenditures and costs. Moreover, the B agencies are likely to be most effective in controlling the unpopular institutions—the proprietary hospitals. A mere restructuring of the B agency is unlikely to instill in it the wisdom and impartiality it takes to regulate health-care delivery needs.

Since overbuilding, duplication, and bad management have been painfully obvious in the hospital industry, the pressure to expand direct government involvement has been irresistible. Broadened powers for the areawide planning agencies and certificate-of-need legislation are two instances of direct intervention. Our view, however, is that the past and current incentive structures facing hospital administrators and other decision makers have contributed to rising costs. No hard evidence suggests that detailed control of hospitals would generate a better set of incentives, and such control has the disadvantage of imposing another layer of administration, with its consequent cost, on the hospital system.

Hospitals are sufficiently complicated institutions to afford a good administrator ways around direct pronouncements. For example, requiring "Bad Samaritan" hospital to close its open-heart surgery unit means nothing if it is still allowed to do thoracic surgery. Where is the dividing line between thoracic surgery and open-heart surgery? Indeed, where is the dividing line between general surgery and thoracic surgery? While persuading—or forcing—a hospital to give up its open-heart surgery capability may be effective, an administrative edict that it give up its open-heart surgery team is unlikely to be effective.

Instead, effort should be directed towards changing the incentives facing decision makers within hospitals so that they are more likely to act in the social interest. A program of decentralized incentives would cost less than detailed regulation, and would almost certainly foster better management since the managers are more familiar with hospital problems and the options open to them.[9] One system of incentives could be embodied in what are called incentive-reimbursement programs.

The issue can be couched somewhat differently—in terms of centralized versus decentralized controls. One way of centralizing the control of hospitals is through certificate-of-need legislation, which gives more power to planning agencies and guarantees that nearly all of a hospital's costs will be reimbursed on a cost-plus basis. Such a system will work better than the current system of decentralized controls (where each administrator and his board make decisions) insofar as the planning agencies make better decisions and the hospitals are administered as competently as they are currently.

The administration of hospitals can be even more centralized, with each hospital reporting directly to a regional or national board (as in the United Kingdom and other countries) that determines not only all capital expenditures but general staffing policies and other controls over operations.

The question of the optimum degree of centralized control is not unique to the hospital industry. Considerable research on the appropriate amount of centralized control has been undertaken in socialist countries as well as in the larger U.S. corporations. In the 1920s, the experience of the U.S.S.R. in planning its economy and of General Motors indicated that complete centralization led to massive inefficiency. Western economists were not surprised at the "brilliant discovery" of Liberman in 1967 that the Soviet economy would work better with more decentralization and with changes in the incentives facing managers.[10]

Our espousal of incentive reimbursement below is an argument that the individual hospital administrator (advised by his staff, his board, the medical staff, and other knowledgeable participants) is the best judge of capital expenditures and of operating policies. We argue that the present system generally has not worked well because the incentives facing the administrator were perverse, motivating higher costs and more elaborate equipment and extensive staff. Changing the incentives to direct the administrator's attention to cost reductions and financial efficiency should do much to improve the situation. This approach is much more promising than greater government control of hospitals.

Incentive Reimbursement. Many of the problems associated with the financing of hospital capital expenditures, as well as those associated with their overall level and distribution, are interrelated with hospital reimbursement policies. Any significant change in the structure of the health-care industry is unlikely the near future; in particular, the greater part of the costs of hospital care will continue to be borne by third parties and most hospital care will continue to be given in nonprofit institutions.

Here, we discuss briefly some of the proposals that have been made for improving reimbursement policies and trace their relations to capital financing.[11]

By general agreement, cost-based reimbursement by third parties has been a significant influence in raising the costs of hospital care. Prospective reimbursement, in one form or another, is a proposed solution endorsed by the American Hospital Association. If reimbursement can be separated from costs, hospital administrators will be motivated to manage the hospital more efficiently, and compromise will be necessary in the continuing demands for extra staff and new equipment and services. Hence such reimbursement is often called "incentive reimbursement."

Some confusion surrounds the purpose of incentive reimbursement. Some people ask: Why should an administrator be paid a bonus to do his job well? Isn't he already paid to do it well? A valid answer is that an administrator faces many constraints and conflicting demands. Incentive reimbursement is a way of resetting his priorities so that the cost and revenue position of the hospital becomes more important to him. Incentive reimbursement does not imply that the average hospital will receive more revenue; it implies only that hospitals will be reimbursed in a way that motivates administrators to hold down costs and manage the financial side of the hospital more efficiently.

A number of formulas have been suggested. Reimbursement could be based on the average cost (per patient or per patient-day) of all hospitals in an area. One variation of this method calls for the average cost to be calculated within narrowly defined groups (both geographically and in terms of teaching programs) to obtain a more "equitable" base for reimbursement. Another proposal involves negotiating a detailed budget with the hospital (which presumably depends on its number of patients or patient-days). A more radical idea is to have individuals contract with the hospital and pay it a capitation fee for future service.[12] Other prospective reimbursement programs will be proposed and implemented under Section 222 of H.R. 1.

In a previous paper, we argued that, to be acceptable, an incentive reimbursement proposal should meet certain criteria.[13] It would have to be considered fair and well designed; in particular, it must consider the types and the number of patients treated, and the extent of the hospital's teaching program. It must also allow hospitals as a group to remain financially viable by covering the cost of equipment and plant.

We proposed a formula that satisfies all of these criteria, since it is based on a cost function that incorporates each explicitly. It can be calibrated to finance any desired rate of cost increase (though low rates might not be perceived as "fair" by the hospitals). It can also meet the full depreciation and interest expenses of the average hospital in the area, and the method and amount of reimbursement would promote rationality in raising new capital. The reimbursement received per diem or per case would cover the cost of providing patient care at an average level of efficiency.[14]

In actuality, some hospitals would be managed less efficiently than average or would have a lower occupancy rate, and hence would incur a deficit. Others would garner a budget surplus.· This formula (and most others) would work so that the hospitals with a surplus—those that have funds to cover expansion of services or modernization—would be those that are either efficiently managed or have high occupancy rates. Hospitals with a deficit would probably be characterized by inefficient administration, low occupancy, or obsolete or expensive plants.

Which hospitals should undertake expansion? Obviously, those with better management or those in areas where the demand is high enough to generate high occupancy rates should do so. Badly managed hospitals would have to change administrators or fold. Those that cannot meet costs because they are in areas of falling demand and low occupancy rates would have to cut back on capacity. Hospitals that are inefficient because of obsolete plant would be encouraged to modernize. If reimbursement included interest and depreciation for the "average" hospital, well-run hospitals that wanted to modernize could borrow funds and pay for the modernization out of future revenues.

To take an extremely simple example, suppose that there are three hospitals in an area, each of which has 500 beds, the same patient mix, and plant of the same age.[15] If the average cost per patient-day is $100, the proposed incentive-reimbursement plan would pay each hospital that amount, no matter what its actual costs were. Suppose that hospital A had costs of $110, because it was inherently inefficient or because it had a low occupancy rate, while hospital C had costs of $90 because it was efficient and heavily utilized. Hospital A would run a deficit of $1.5 million while hospital C would have a surplus of that amount. Clearly, hospital A would have to become more efficient, cut staff to match its lower rate, merge, or go bankrupt. Hospital C would be accumulating funds that it could use for expansion and modernization. If the hospitals were equally efficient but hospital A was in an area of declining population while hospital C was in one that was expanding, the deficit and surplus would be the proper signal to hospital A to cut its staff to a level commensurate with its service and to hospital C to expand its plant to accommodate the greater demand.

A proposal such as this would tie capital expenditures to current operations. It therefore would tend to use market criteria to govern which hospitals expand and which survive. The term "market criteria" is slightly misleading since negotiations with the government, unions, and other employing agencies will affect the decisions about illnesses and treatment processes to be reimbursed by these third parties. This proposal is radically different from one that would submit capital expenditures to the mercies of planning agencies.[16] It does not deny a fruitful role to the planning agencies, since they are admirably structured to represent the desires of the community. Their preponderance of consumer representatives and their representatives of the institutions and professionals associated with health-care delivery give them excellent sources of information about the desires of all parties for new facilities and programs, even if they are not structured to sort out these desires and transform them into working plans.

Difficulties with Incentive Reimbursement

Three situations seem to present problems to the incentive-reimbursement system we propose. The first is the well-managed hospital that is the right size to service its area, but that keeps running an embarrassing budget surplus. The second is the establishment of a new hospital or the complete modernization of an existing hospital that runs a deficit because an obsolete plant makes its operations very expensive. The third is the ghetto hospital. These are treated in turn.

The Embarrassing Budget Surplus. If a hospital that provides excellent service to its area and that has no reason to expand is managed more efficiently than average, it will generate budget surpluses.

What can they be used for? There are four alternatives: (1) expansion, which would cause the occupancy rate of the hospital to fall and put a stop to surpluses; (2) acquisition of new—unneeded—equipment or new services, which would also have the effect of curtailing future surpluses; (3) accumulation of surpluses toward plant modernization; or (4) aggressive expansion of outpatient, community, emergency, or teaching services. If the hospital were administered well enough to generate a surplus, one suspects that it would resist doing something to increase costs with little improvement in service.[17]

Establishing a New Hospital. The Hill-Burton agencies have concluded that although there is some need for relocating existing hospitals, the total number of beds need not be expanded. Population growth and shift imply the need for new beds in growing metropolitan areas and a reduction of beds in declining areas. The net result is a limited need for new hospitals.

A new hospital (or new plant for an obsolete, deficit-ridden hospital) might be financed by philanthropy, federal grants, or a loan. Under a Hill-Burton program, reformed third-party financing, or certificate-of-need legislation, it would be extremely difficult to prove the need for a new hospital and obtain approval and funding.

The incentive-reimbursement proposal would provide an interesting alternative. Under this proposal, backers of a new hospital need only convince a financial institution that they could pay the interest and amortization on the loan. If their forecast of sufficient demand proves correct and if they can run the hospital efficiently, they will be able to meet the obligation. If they are wrong, they will have to cover the deficit or the financial institution will lose. The appropriate analogy is to an entrepreneur's attempt to borrow the capital to set up a business. We suspect that the incentive-reimbursement plan would provide a more rationally located and run network of hospitals than the alternatives of Hill-Burton funds, third-party reimbursement that covers incurred costs, or certificates of need.

The Ghetto Hospital. A different sort of problem arises for the hospital whose clientele includes a high proportion of bad-debt (or free-care) patients. However efficiently it is run and however high its occupancy rates, such a hospital may never be able to generate the funds to modernize or expand. Even the enactment of Medicaid has not overcome this difficulty, since most states have limited programs that fail to cover many of the medically indigent. The potential magnitude of this problem is plain in the proportion of the population under 65 in various income classes with hospital insurance, as shown in Table 17.

One means of assisting these hospitals is government grants for needed modernization or expansion. Another is an attempt to reduce the burden of free care by cutting down the number of medically indigent patients, either by extending the Medicaid program or through a publicly supported insurance program (with incentive reimbursement). This approach is the superior one for the same reasons cited above. However, such a widespread reform in the financing of hospitalization expenditures for low-income people may be impossible to carry out. If so, there is no alternative to government grants.

Table 17

DISTRIBUTION OF POPULATION UNDER 65 WITH HOSPITAL INSURANCE, BY INCOME, 1968

Income	Percent
Under $3,000	36.3
$3,000–$4,999	56.8
5,000– 6,999	78.5
7,000– 9,999	89.3
10,000 or more	92.3
Total, all income classes	80.3

Source: Department of Health, Education and Welfare, Social Security Administration, *Medical Care Costs and Prices,* (SSA) 72-11908, January 1972, p. 97.

While no good evidence exists on the number of hospitals in this situation, it cannot be very large. Virtually all of the population is covered by some form of hospital insurance, by Medicare, or by Medicaid. Municipal or other government-supported hospitals generally provide care in areas where substantial numbers of individuals are not insured and cannot afford to pay for care. Since the states are responsible for defining the coverage and reimbursement policies of Medicaid, they should supply the remedy for any problem that arises from definitions that fail to cover hospital costs.

Summary

At present, hospitals find it easy to cover operating expenses but very difficult to finance capital projects such as expansion and modernization (neglecting the effects of the price freeze). The vast increase in hospitalization insurance means that the great majority of patients are covered and that the hospital is reimbursed for their care by third parties on a cost-plus basis. Philanthropy and government grants cover only a small portion of their capital needs, so hospitals must rely on revenues from patient services to finance capital projects. The capital needs of hospitals exceed $1.5 billion a year, only a small fraction of which can be covered by a program such as Hill-Burton. This means that capital expenditures are inextricably linked to the complicated reimbursement formulas used by Blue Cross, Medicare, and Medicaid. While grants under the Hill-Burton program make it easier for a hospital to modernize, the cost of capital projects must be borne, in large part, by philanthropy and additional charges to self-pay patients. The shift of the Hill-Burton program to loan guarantees has little justification and is likely to prove costly to the government in terms of high default rates.

The only likely source of funds for capital expenditures is revenue from services to patients. Payment of depreciation and interest costs by third parties, however, would essentially guarantee that a hospital could cover the costs of an expansion, whether it served the community or not. Strict controls on hospitals would be required to prevent needless capital expenditures.

Giving more control to planning agencies, such as the areawide Comprehensive Health Planning Agencies (B agencies), is one way to prevent needless expansion. These agencies already have substantial power in the certificates of need they issue, giving their approval for any capital expenditure over a minimal amount, which is reinforced by their power to deny reimbursement to hospitals under federal patient-care programs if capital expenditures are undertaken without their approval.

The B agencies are not structured to perform these control and approval tasks well, however. Indeed, we doubt that any agency could do so in the face of political pressure and demands from the providers of health care. The B agencies have not yet succeeded in performing these functions, and few experts predict success in the near future.

The perverse incentives embodied in the present system have played a major role in the rapid increase in hospitalization costs, in underutilization of facilities, and in bad patient care. Cost-plus reimbursement has shifted the hospital administrator's attention from controlling costs and running the hospital efficiently to satisfying the demands of his medical staff and his board for more elaborate facilities.

Incentive reimbursement would create incentives that would direct attention to the costs and revenues of the hospital. As such, it would shift power from the medical staff to the hospital administrator and shift the emphasis from the desire for the newest and most elaborate medical equipment and specialty staff to management control and evaluation. Incentive reimbursement can take many forms from negotiated budgets to the setting of rates determined by the services provided by the hospital. We advocate the latter approach and propose a formula that relies on a negotiated rate of overall cost increase with an adjustment for the case-mix actually served. This reimbursement plan would do much to reform incentives within the hospital and would be helpful in lowering costs and improving patient care.

Three problems might arise under our proposal. The first is an embarrassing budget surplus to a well-managed hospital, which would accumulate for future capital expenditures or be spent for expanded services. The second is the modernization of an existing hospital, or the establishment of a new one, whose board would have to convince a financial institution to lend it funds, with amortization and interest coming from future patient revenues. The third is the ghetto hospital with a high proportion of free-care patients, which would require government grants for capital projects. None of these problems poses substantial difficulties, in our view.

Current legislation (P.L. 92-603, generally known as H.R. 1) requires the government to conduct and evaluate experiments in incentive reimbursement of hospitals. It is crucial that these experiments be well designed and conducted to provide guidance on the possibilities and problems of this approach. If the experiments are poorly designed or if they merely imitate the current system, not only will funds be wasted, but policy makers will fail to get essential evidence on the workability of incentive reimbursement. We emphasize the need for good experiments and note the difficulty of conducting them. Much work will have to be done to ensure that this precious opportunity is not wasted.

NOTES

NOTES TO INTRODUCTION

[1] The program has subsidized short-term (acute) hospitals, long-term (mental, tuberculosis, rehabilitation, et cetera) hospitals and ambulatory-care facilities. The term "health facilities" will refer to all these institutions; "long-term hospitals" will refer to inpatient facilities whose average length of stay exceeds thirty days; "hospitals" (occasionally "short-term hospitals" for emphasis) will refer only to short-stay institutions; total hospitals will refer to long- and short-term hospitals.

[2] This is a selective history and evaluation, focusing on amendments affecting the level and type of construction supported under the program. Other activities—such as research in hospital administration and hospital design, demonstration projects on utilization control, and areawide planning—have been supported.

NOTES TO CHAPTER I

[1] Commission on Hospital Care, *Hospital Care in the United States: A Study of the Function of the General Hospital, Its Role in the Care of All Types of Illnesses, and the Conduct of Activities Related to Patient Service, with Recommendations for its Extension and Integration for More Adequate Care of the American Public* (New York: Commonwealth Fund, 1947).

[2] U.S. Congress, Senate, *Hearings before a Subcommittee of the Committee on Education and Labor on S. 3230*, 76th Congress, 2d session, 1940, and *Hearings before the Committee on Education and Labor on S. 191*, 79th Congress, 1st session, 1945.

[3] P.L. 83-482.

[4] Harris-Hill Amendments, P.L. 88-443.

[5] P.L. 91-296.

[6] We have discussed the efficacy of increased expenditures on medical care elsewhere (J. Lave and L. Lave, "Medical Care and Its Delivery: An Economic Appraisal," *Law and Contemporary Problems*, vol. 35 [Spring 1970], pp. 252-266), and merely wish to note that health indices, such as life expectancy and infant and maternal mortality rates, do not indicate that the vast increases in expenditure on medical services have worked to improve health.

In terms of the allocation of resources in the delivery of health care, we note that hospital care is but one input into the health production process. Its use will depend on the supply of other factors and on the incentives facing patients and physicians. Utilization rates differ substantially for prepaid group practice versus fee-for-service practice. Where hospital beds are plentiful and physicians scarce, one would expect to see higher hospital rates and fewer ambulatory visits per capita. Evidence on the effect of cleaner environment and other factors on the health of the population can be found in L. Lave and E. Seskin, "Air Pollution and Human Health," *Science,* vol. 169 (August 21, 1969), pp. 723-733; R. Auster, I. Leveson and D. Sarachek, "The Production of Health: An Exploratory Study," *The Journal of Human Resources,* vol. 4 (Fall 1969), pp. 412-436; and J. Lave and S. Leinhardt, "The Delivery of Ambulatory Care to the Poor: A Literature Review," *Management Science,* vol. 19 (December 1972), pp. 78-99.

[7] See *Federal Register,* vol. 37, no. 3, part 2 (January 6, 1972), pp. 182-193, for rules and regulations governing grant support and loan guarantees under the Hill-Burton program.

[8] Public Health Service Act, Title VI, Section 603.

[9] Adapted from the example presented by Paul A. Brinker and Burley Walker, "The Hill Burton Act: 1948-1954," *Review of Economics and Statistics,* vol. 44 (May 1962), p. 210.

[10] Statement of John Veneman, undersecretary of HEW, in *Hearings before the Subcommittee on Health of the Committee on Labor and Public Welfare on S. 2182,* U.S. Senate, 91st Congress, 1st session (1969), pp. 230-231.

NOTES TO CHAPTER II

[1] U.S. Department of Health, Education and Welfare, *Hill-Burton Project Register,* 1 July 1947—30 June 1971 (Washington, D. C.: U.S. Government Printing Office, 1972).

[2] Not all the projects involving modernization were financed through the specific modernization grant program. Considerable modernization was undertaken through the general construction program.

[3] The law permits states that do not use their full allotments to transfer their unused portion to other states. Low-income states, therefore, may not in fact have received proportionately more funds. We have no data on the extent to which allotted funds were not fully used but would infer from the data in the text that it was limited.

[4] There were 590 hospitals in our sample, a number of which had more than one Hill-Burton project. On average, each hospital benefited from 1.5 projects.

[5] These data do not permit inferences about the kinds of income distribution involved because there are no data on the distribution of families by counties according to county incomes.

[6] U.S. Department of Health, Education and Welfare, *General Standards of Construction and Equipment for Hospital and Medical Facilities* (Washington, D. C.: U.S. Government Printing Office, 1969).

[7] Public Health Service Act, Title VI, Section 605(a)(5).

[8] Comptroller General of the United States, *Study of Health Facilities Construction Costs* (Washington, D. C.: U.S. Government Printing Office, 1972).

[9] Ibid., p. 22.

[10] These findings are presented and discussed in John P. Gould, *Davis-Bacon Act: The Economics of Prevailing Wage Laws* (Washington, D. C.: American Enterprise Institute for Public Policy Research, 1971).

[11] Paul S. Pierson, "GAO Studies Construction Costs," *Hospitals,* Journal of the American Medical Association, vol. 47 (February 1, 1973), p. 52.

[12] We interviewed about ten hospital administrators in a number of states about the additional cost that might arise from the Hill-Burton requirements, and in general their answers corresponded with the findings of the GAO. All of them claimed that they had studied the problem with care on recent construction projects and had concluded that the requirements increased cost of construction about 5-30 percent.

[13] *Federal Register,* vol. 37, no. 142 (July 22, 1972).

NOTES TO CHAPTER III

[1] In 1948 a state had to determine only whether the beds constituted a public hazard. By 1964, explicit federal minimum standards had been set. Conforming beds are those that meet these standards.

[2] These data are all from U.S. Department of Health, Education and Welfare, *Health Facilities Existing and Needed—Hill-Burton State Plan Data as of 1969* (Washington, D. C.: U.S. Government Printing Office, 1971).

[3] Martin S. Feldstein, "The Welfare Loss of Excess Hospital Insurance," *Journal of Political Economy,* vol. 81, no. 2, pt. 1 (March/April 1973), pp. 251-280.

[4] See Milton I. Roemer et al., *Health Insurance Effects,* Bureau of Public Economics, Research Series No. 16, School of Public Health (Ann Arbor: The University of Michigan, 1972). The finding of different hospital utilization rates has often been duplicated and is one of the reasons why the health maintenance organization concept gets so much support.

[5] Comptroller General of the United States, *Study of Health Facilities Construction Costs* (Washington, D. C.: U.S. Government Printing Office, 1972). These kinds of studies indicate once again the elusive nature of the concept of "need." Given the possibility that the opportunity cost of physicians is much higher in some rural areas, it may make sense there to hospitalize people who do not require it to conserve this scarce resource.

[6] All data on number of hospital beds come from the "Hospital Guide Issue," *Hospitals,* vol. 22 (August 1971). Total beds include all those in reporting hospitals; short-term hospital beds are beds in hospitals in which over 50 percent of all patients admitted stay less than thirty days. Short-term beds include all the so-called general hospital beds in the United States. Total hospital beds do *not* include those in nursing homes, which are counted with the long-term beds in the Hill-Burton state plan data discussed above.

[7] See Chapter IV for a more detailed description of the unique role of a Hill-Burton grant in financing construction.

[8] Note that the exact cost of an extra bed varies directly with the estimated regression coefficient and so must be calculated for the regression of particular interest.

[9] The Hill-Burton data come from the one-fifth sample of general hospitals ever receiving support under the Hill-Burton program, which we described in Chapter II.

[10] Forty-two hospitals in the one-fifth sample are missing from this tabulation. Some have probably closed their doors; others changed their names or merged with other hospitals to form more efficient units. In 1970, 55 percent of all short-term hospitals had less than 100 beds; 45 percent of the sampled Hill-Burton units and 43 percent of all nongovernment, nonproprietary hospitals were in this category.

[11] T. Parran in *Hearings before the Committee on Education and Labor on S. 191,* U.S. Senate, 79th Congress, 1st session, pp. 57-58.

[12] V. Fuchs and M. Kramer, *Determinants of Expenditures for Physicians' Services in the United States 1948-1968,* National Bureau of Economic Research Paper 117 (Washington, D. C.: U.S. Government Printing Office, 1973).

[13] Robert Kaplan and Samuel Leinhardt, "The Determinants of Physician Office Location," *Medical Care,* vol. 11 (September/October 1973).

[14] L. Benham, A. Maurizi, and M. Reder, "Migration, Location and Remuneration of Medical Personnel: Physicians and Dentists," *Review of Economics and Statistics,* vol. 50 (August 1968), pp. 332-347.

[15] Two sets of data are available for the number of physicians in each state in 1950. They are highly correlated, although not the same. We have looked at both and find little difference in their implications for the analysis.

[16] B. Peter Pashigian finds that "the Hill-Burton program has raised the measured index of room rates." *The Hill-Burton Program: The Effects of the Federal Subsidy in Kind on the Hospital Industry* (Report 7346, Center for Mathematical Studies in Business and Economics, University of Chicago, 1973), p. 12.

[17] Richard L. Johnson, "Proprietary Capital: A Report of the 1967 National Forum on Hospital and Health Affairs," in *Hearings before the Subcommittee on Health of the Committee on Labor and Public Welfare on S. 2182,* U.S. Senate, 91st Congress, 1st session (1969), p. 207.

[18] Bruce Steinwald and Duncan Neuhauser, "The Role of the Proprietary Hospital," *Law and Contemporary Problems,* vol. 35 (Autumn 1970), pp. 817-838.

NOTES TO CHAPTER IV

[1] The remaining 3.7 percent came from other internal funding sources. American Hospital Association, "Research Capsules No. 5," *Hospitals,* vol. 46 (March 1, 1972), pp. 184-185.

[2] A modernization program does not lead to a decrease in costs because it is usually accompanied by an expansion in the quantity and quality of services offered, and thus almost always increases costs.

[3] We have simplified the reimbursement procedure of Blue Cross of Western Pennsylvania. The reimbursement procedure being discussed is the most common one, but current alternatives include a negotiated budget and a type of prospective reimbursement.

[4] See Herman M. Somers and Anne R. Somers, *Medicine and the Hospitals* (Washington, D. C.: The Brookings Institution, 1967).

[5] Actually, in some states it is suggested that the planning agencies also review operating expenses. Since this paper was written a number of alternative proposals have been set forth. For example, in the state of Maryland the Health Services Cost Review Commission has been given the authority to set all rates for each hospital. If capital projects are deemed necessary by the commission for a particular hospital, its rates will be set correspondingly higher.

[6] D. Brown, "The Process of Areawide Planning: Model for the Future," *Medical Care* (January-February 1973), p. 10.

[7] See P.L. 89-749, Section 314.

[8] See, for example, Edmund W. Kitch, "Regulation of the Field Market for Natural Gas by the Federal Power Commission," *The Journal of Law and Economics,* vol. 11 (October 1968), pp. 243-280; Edmund W. Kitch, Marc Isaacson, and Daniel Kasper, "The Regulation of Taxicabs in Chicago," *The Journal of Law and Economics,* vol. 14 (October 1971), pp. 285-350; P. MacAvoy and J. Sloss, *Regulation of Transport Innovation* (New York: Random House, 1967); and Ann F. Friedlaender, *The Dilemma of Freight Transport Regulation* (Washington, D. C.: The Brookings Institution, 1969).

[9] John M. Mecklin, "Hospitals Need Management Even More than Money," *Fortune,* vol. 83 (January 1970), pp. 96-99, 150-151.

[10] Y. Liberman, "The Plan, Profits and Bonuses," in *The Soviet Economy: A Book of Readings,* ed. M. Bornstein and D. Fusfeld (Homewood, Ill.: Richard D. Irwin, Inc., 1970).

[11] Solutions other than prospective reimbursement have been advocated. One is the development of health maintenance organizations. A person would contract with an HMO for all of the medical services he needs and pay a capitation fee. The system would encourage much more efficient use of the hospital. With the medical system vertically integrated in this manner, the most efficient way to meet the hospital's costs becomes a major problem.

[12] C. Patrick Hardwick, Susan B. Meyers and Linnis Woodruff, *Incentive Reimbursement: Prospects, Proposals, Plans and Programs*, Research Series Number 6 (Blue Cross of Western Pennsylvania, February 1969).

[13] Judith R. Lave, Lester B. Lave and Lester P. Silverman, "A Proposal for Incentive Reimbursement for Hospitals," *Medical Care*, vol. 11 (March 1973), pp. 79-90.

[14] Such a formula could also be used to pay proprietary hospitals for care rendered to patients covered by government programs or Blue Cross. It would answer one criticism of the proprietary hospitals—that they skim off the cream—for a formula based on actual case mix would pay much less to hospitals serving less costly patients. The formula would have to be periodically re-estimated.

[15] If the area needed only 1,200 beds, the current Hill-Burton regulations would call for the modernization of the first 500 beds of the first hospitals applying, thus tending to confirm the number of excess beds.

[16] There will always be the problem of the introduction of experimental equipment into some hospitals—generally teaching hospitals. General reimbursement formulas usually will not cover these costs.

[17] Alternatively, the superior services of the managers would be rewarded through higher salaries as they were bid away.